Also by Brigitte van Tuijl

*The Gap - bridge the space between where
you are and where you want to be
The Inner Minimalist - clear the clutter of your
mind for a simpler, quieter and happier life
Write Your Non-Fiction Book in 3 Months (in only 30 minutes per day)*

The Art of Divine Selfishness Series

Book One: *Unmute Your Life - break free from
fear & go for what you REALLY want*
Book Two: *The Art of Divine Selfishness - transform your
life, your business & the world by putting YOU first*

Books in Dutch

Ontdek Wat Je Écht Wilt En Maak Daar (Je) Werk Van

the Happy Hermit

HOW TO THRIVE
AS AN INTROVERT ENTREPRENEUR

BRIGITTE VAN TUIJL

BOOK 3 IN THE 'THE ART OF DIVINE SELFISHNESS' SERIES

ISBN Paperback: 978-90-832226-0-8

ISBN e-book: 978-90-832226-1-5

Visit www.booksbybrigitte.com for more books by the author.

For additional gifts, visit www.bookfreebees.com

The information provided in this book is designed to inspire, educate, motivate, and enlighten you on the subjects discussed. It's not meant as a substitute for professional coaching or other expert assistance. If such level of assistance is required, please seek the services of a competent professional or contact the author directly for one-to-one coaching options. The author assumes no liability for use of the information and exercises.

Copy editor: Kelly Urgan
Cover design: Susan D. Johnson

Contents

**Part Three—Practical Tips to Make Your
Business Introvert Friendly**

Part Four—Troubleshooting

Introduction

For years, I struggled with being extremely introverted. Not that I knew what that was. No one did. All I knew was that I wanted to read a book and be alone when I came home from school. I didn't know I needed that because I'd been around people all day and needed solitude to recharge—a fundamental characteristic of introverts.

Over the years, I tried to find a balance between interaction with others and being on my own. I never had quite enough time to myself, but I managed as best I could. Weekdays were filled with school and later work, so I tried to find as much alone time as possible in the evenings and weekends. But I never found enough solitude in my work. I worked in an office and was surrounded by people all day. I liked the people I worked with, but being around them was still draining.

When I started my business in 2003, I felt so relieved. Freedom! Finally, I could have all the time in the world to be alone! That didn't turn out exactly as I hoped, as you can read in the first part of this book. I worked as a coach and loved my work. (Still do.) I loved my clients and having my own business. But something was off. *Either* I had plenty of clients and made enough money but I didn't have enough alone time, *or* I had fewer clients, enjoyed my space and solitude, but I didn't make enough money. I didn't like this unhappy cycle. But I figured that was just the way things were. I thought it was the price I had to pay for being an introvert. So I was grateful for everything I had and enjoyed that as best I could. I was still *massively* better off than ever before in my life, and I was thankful for that.

In 2011, I changed my business and basically started a new one: I quit working as a career coach, stopped working in Dutch, and started working internationally, in English, with women entrepreneurs. A completely new phase started! My new business was a success from the start and I loved my work. Still, something felt off again. I noticed the same thing had happened: my business was doing well and I made enough money, but I didn't have enough alone time. Even though my schedule wasn't full (especially compared with other coaches), it still felt too busy for me.

But something had changed. I was no longer willing to settle for anything less than what I *truly* wanted. I was no longer willing to accept that feeling drained was the price of being introverted. I no longer accepted that I had to choose between having enough money OR having enough alone time. I decided to have both and to create a business that was 100 percent ideal for me, instead of 90 percent ideal. Why settle for anything less?

I decided to turn myself from a crappy hermit to a happy hermit. And that's what I did. I explored how much freedom and space I *truly* wanted, and did whatever it took to make that ideal picture my reality. For me, this means I make a maximum of four appointments per week, three weeks per month. Every fourth week is my hermit week, my completely appointment-free week. I hardly ever set an alarm clock. I don't make plans. I follow my intuition and flow in each moment, and I have all the time and space in the world.

In this book, I share how I created a business and life I adore without compromising or changing who I am. And I show you how *you* can do the same, whether or not you're an introvert like me. The book IS specifically meant for introverts, though. **I find it extremely important to show introverts that they *really do not have to change ANYTHING about themselves*.** Extroverts are still the norm in our (western) world, and introverts *always* get the message, implicitly or explicitly, that they should change or adjust themselves to what's considered "normal." We're told not to be so shy, to speak up more, to make ourselves more visible. We have to do projects with others in school and at work. We're told that we're no fun when we want to be on our own or leave a party early. We're constantly told how we should change. Even some people who specifically aim their coaching or books at introverts tell us how to adjust ourselves. They give tips on how to survive networking events instead of telling us you don't have to go at all. They tell us how to get through the holidays without feeling drained instead of teaching us how to decline invitations and prioritize our need for alone time over pleasing others.

You won't find ANY of that in my book. On the contrary!! I believe that the more you are true to yourself and your true nature, the better you feel AND the more successful you are. (Whatever "success" means to you!) You NEVER have to change yourself to fulfill your purpose and live your true dreams. You NEVER have to change who you are to fit in or to accommodate others. You don't have to adjust your behavior because the world decided that extrovert behavior is the norm.

This book is a testament to STOP changing yourself or sacrificing your sanity for any reason. This book is an ode to all introverts and to doing everything in your own way, on your own terms. I hope it inspires you to embrace ALL that you are and build your entire business and life around your true self.

Love,

Brigitte

Are You An Introvert, Too?

You probably identify as an introvert, or you wouldn't be reading this book. But what exactly *is* an introvert? And what characterizes an extrovert?

In general, introverts are more focused on their own inner world, their thoughts, ideas, and feelings, rather than seeking external stimulation. Interaction with and being around others is often draining, even when they love the people they're with. Introverts recharge by being alone.

Being introverted does NOT mean that you're shy! Shyness indicates a fear of people or social situations. That's something completely different. You can be a shy extrovert, and you can be an outspoken, sometimes loudmouthed introvert. (That would be me. ;-))

Extroverts, on the other hand, thrive off interaction. Social events leave them feeling renewed and energized. They enjoy groups and group work, and feel isolated if they spend too much time alone. They look to outside sources for ideas and inspiration, whereas introverts find this in their own inner world. Extroverts recharge by being around people.

There are also ambiverts, who are equal parts introverted and extroverted.

These are generalizations, of course, and one personality trait alone doesn't identify who you are. So please take all of this with a grain of salt. Yes, it can be liberating to discover what type of person you are or what label you can put on your character or personality.

Just don't get attached to any labels or definitions. There's only ONE mold you fit into completely: your own.

Get to know yourself, your needs, wants, and dreams as best you can. These tell you more about yourself than any label or definition ever can. You are *truly unique*, even when you share certain traits with others. Introvert, extrovert, and ambivert are just labels. They never do *all* of you justice, and it's certainly not who you truly are! (Who you truly are is a soul having a human experience, a spark of the divine; you are pure consciousness expressing itself in human form.)

Still, it's good to know if you're more introverted or extroverted. It can help you understand how you perceive the world. It can help you take better care of yourself, and it can help you get to know yourself better. For that reason, here's a list of characteristics that are commonly attributed to introverts. Read through this list and see how many statements resonate with you. This gives you an idea of how introverted you are.

- Socializing, human interaction and being around people (even when you love them) drain your energy.
- You enjoy spending time alone.
- You do your best thinking (and brainstorming) alone.
- You can feel lonelier in a crowd than on your own.
- You need time to process information and input before you can respond. That's why brainstorming with others or making decisions on the spot is usually not your forte. You need some space to chew on your thoughts and feelings.
- You don't like to be the center of attention.
- When you socialize too much, you shut down. You're peopled out! You need to be alone to recharge. If you don't get that solitude, you can get irritated.
- You have a couple of close friends. Because spending time with people drains you, you're *very* mindful of who you spend your time with.

- You don't need a massive amount of stimuli to feel energized. Extroverts love busyness. They thrive on it! You don't. It's too loud, too much, and extra draining. Reading a book or enjoying your inner world is entertaining enough for you!
- You're a good listener.
- Others often ask for your input or opinion. That's because you're observant and carefully process information. When you say something, it's generally spot on!
- You prefer communicating via email instead of by phone. That way, you have no direct interaction and can choose when to respond to messages.
- Too much stimulation overloads your system. It distracts you and leaves you unfocused. It's overwhelming.
- You have good self-knowledge. You're used to introspection and reflection, and self-awareness and self-knowledge are the natural result of that.
- You prefer learning through reading or observing something first (as opposed to extroverts who learn by doing). You rather prepare yourself before you jump in.
- Others often think you're quiet.
- You don't like small talk, but you LOVE deep conversations.
- You usually think before you speak or act.

I consider myself to be extremely introverted, because I need *a lot* of alone time to feel happy and fulfilled. This is why I started calling myself a hermit in 2012.

What is Divine Selfishness?!

This is the third book in The Art of Divine Selfishness series. So, what exactly is Divine Selfishness, and how does this book fit in?

Divine Selfishness means to put your soul first. To live the life your soul chose to experience. To live YOUR life—instead of a life others want, or expect—you to live. To do that, you need to put yourself first: your needs, wants, desires, and your truth, which is, of course, the selfish part of Divine Selfishness. The divine part has to do with the fact that you put your *soul* first. You come from your *heart*. When you do this, you automatically contribute to the well-being of all.

The universe doesn't make mistakes. Every living being has a place and a purpose, which is ALWAYS to contribute to the whole. When you put your soul first, when you put *yourself* first, you automatically serve others. You serve others by being who you truly are and doing what you most love! Just like bees and bananas have their place in life and contribute to it by simply being who they are.

Being Divinely Selfish means you can serve without suffering, without changing who you are, without doing things you hate. Being Divinely Selfish is quite the contrary! You follow your joy, your heart, the path your soul lays out for you.

This differs vastly from the selfishness that comes from fear, lack, neediness, or greed. Shallow self-centeredness serves only one person: you. Selfishness is disconnected from the heart, from the soul, from love. But Divine Selfishness? Serves all.

The first book in this series, *Unmute Your Life - break free from fear & go for what you REALLY want*, focuses on uncovering your true dreams and making them real.

The second book, *The Art of Divine Selfishness - transform your life, your business & the world by putting YOU first*, focuses on prioritizing yourself and your dreams. It teaches you the mindset and practical skills you need to put your soul first, prioritize your self-care, and pursue your true dreams.

This third book in the Art of Divine Selfishness series shows you how to thrive as an introvert entrepreneur. You need to build your business around yourself, your dreams, your wants and your needs, so you can blossom. You can only thrive when you prioritize yourself and make who you *really* are the foundation of your business.

PART ONE

My Journey

From Crappy Hermit to Happy Hermit

Introduction

Part One describes my journey from crappy hermit to happy hermit. I walk you through the steps I took, the fears I had, the things that worked and the things that were hard.

If you dream of creating a business and life that are completely ideal for you, my story can inspire you. To help you harvest insights and clarity, I end each chapter with a couple of reflective questions (**Introvert Introspections**) for you to journal on. Some of these questions are repeated in different ways throughout the book. There are two reasons for this repetition. First, you may not read every chapter. Repeating some key questions throughout the book increases the chance that you'll reflect on these important inquiries. Second, new answers and insights can come up when a question is asked in a slightly different way or from a different perspective.

Pay attention to the parts of my story that speak to you, and the parts that don't. Ask yourself: what is it that speaks to me? What is it that I like or dislike? What does this tell me about what *I* need to thrive?

I share my story in Part One in chronological order, so it's best to read the chapters in the order they're in, but feel free to read the rest of the book however you want. Do it *your* way, as I invite you to do EVERYTHING in your business and life. ;-)

Chapter 1

Before I Started My Business

I have always needed a lot of alone time. I was happiest when I was on my own, immersed in a book.

I didn't know I was introverted. I didn't even know what that was! No one did. It wasn't a thing when I was growing up. I only knew that when I came home from school, I wanted to be on my own.

People around me didn't always understand or like that. They thought I was anti-social. Or selfish. My mother warned me that if I kept saying "no" to invitations to play outside, children would stop inviting me one day. I didn't care. So what? I wanted to be left alone and read books anyway.

People were often disappointed when I didn't show up at a party or I didn't want to take part in a social activity. But I learned to stop letting their disappointment get to me. The price of ignoring my needs was simply too high!

By the time I got my first job, I knew how to make sure I had enough energy in my personal life, even though I was surrounded by people all week. My coping strategies weren't very healthy, though: with alcohol and cigarettes I formed a literal and energetic screen between me and others. This screen closed me off from others' energies and drama. Later, I learned to keep my energy high by grounding myself and clearing my energy field, so I no longer needed cigarettes or alcohol. I also became a pro at saying "no" and setting boundaries to protect the alone time I so desperately needed.

By the time I quit my last job and started my business in 2003, my *personal* life was completely hermit-friendly: I never made more than one appointment per weekend and sometimes an additional appointment during the week. My partner and I were always together, but since we each had our own place, I could be alone if I wanted to.

My *work life*, however, did NOT give me the alone time I needed during the week. So when I quit my job and started my business on July 1, I was over the moon happy. At last! Freedom! No more people around me all day, every day! I couldn't be happier.

Introvert Introspections:

- Do you have enough time to recharge and be alone?
- What would that ideally look like?
- If your life doesn't look like that yet, what needs to change?

Chapter 2

The Start of My Business—The Dream

I had a very clear image of what my ideal business and workweek looked like:

I was at home, doing my own thing, day in day out. A couple of times per week, I coached a client to find their purpose in a job. At the end of the month, I sent out invoices. And I lived happily ever after.

It was a simple dream. And during the summer of 2003, I lived most of that dream. I was home alone. I created dozens of cool coaching exercises and read tons of books. For the first time in my life, I had a lot of space and alone time. I had never had enough solitude in my work life, and I made up for that now! I did the opposite of what most people do when they start their business: I turned inward and stayed inside, both literally and figuratively. Most people turn outward when they start their business. They talk to others, create a website, and do whatever they can to find clients. I did the opposite. I completely withdrew from the world—and I never felt happier. :-)

I didn't connect with people. I didn't have a website—I only created that two years later. I didn't network, and I didn't do any marketing. I enjoyed my alone time and everything I'd never had enough time for. I was living my dream!

The *only* part of the dream that hadn't come true yet was coaching clients. But that was okay. I had enough money to get me through the summer.

In September, I found my first client, and two months later my second client showed up. I was so happy! I did purposeful work I deeply loved and made enough money to pay the bills. I had plenty of alone time for the first time in my life, and I'd built my business around myself, my needs and my desires from the start:

I didn't make any appointments before 10 a.m. or after 5 p.m.

I worked with my ideal clients only (instead of working with anyone with a pulse and a question—like many coaches do, especially when they are just starting out).

I loved my work.

I never felt better!

Introvert Introspections:

- When you started your business, what did your dream day / week look like?
- Does your reality look like that?
- If not, what do you think needs to change to make that happen?

Chapter 3

The Start of My Business—
The Reality

The first three clients came to me effortlessly. My former employer referred my first client. The second client was a former colleague who contacted me. And a friend referred my third client. I was grateful. This was easy!

But after that third client, it became harder. No one came to me and I had NO clue what to do to get clients. I knew nothing about marketing. And honestly? I didn't *want* to do any marketing. Partly because the idea of making myself visible scared the living daylights out of me. And partly because I enjoyed my alone time too much. I was still making up for lost (alone) time.

But something needed to change. No clients meant no money, and that was not a sustainable way to live. I borrowed some money, which tided me over until the next client magically came along. After that it I had to borrow some more money. I *just* made ends meet until the next client came along.

I was still super happy with my solitude. But the financial stress and insecurity made me miserable. After a year and a half, I realized I couldn't go on like this. I saw only two options: to learn about marketing and how to get clients, or give up my business and go back to a job.

The latter was not an option. Just *thinking* about it made me want to throw up. Reluctantly, I signed up for a marketing workshop. I didn't want to, but I didn't see an alternative. I also found a temporary part-time job. That didn't make me happy either, but I needed the money. I was committed to doing what it took to get my business off the ground.

Introvert Introspections:

- What, if anything, about your business makes you extremely happy?
- How could you expand on the things that make you happy?
- What, if anything, do you dislike about your business?
- What step(s) do you know deep down you have to take to solve those things?

Chapter 4

The Unhappy Cycle

Slowly but surely, I got the hang of marketing. I learned how to get ideal clients in ways that felt good to me. My business grew. I wrote my first book, and it sold well. I finally mastered being an entrepreneur and making money. Yay, me! I was grateful and happy.

But …

There was a downside to my success. I had too many appointments, had too much interaction, and saw too many people. I said "no" as often as I could. But if I wanted to make enough money, I had to have sales conversations and work with people one-to-one.

Every time my schedule felt too busy, I said "no" to new clients. And every time, the same thing happened: I had fewer appointments and more alone time, which made me happy. But I also had fewer clients and made less money. This stressed me out and made me unhappy. When the stress got to be too much and I needed more money, I started working with more clients. This solved the money problem, but also resulted in a schedule that was too crowded again.

This unhappy cycle continued for years. I had *either* enough money *or* enough alone time, but I never enjoyed both simultaneously.

I tried to break this cycle by adding group coaching programs to my services. This helped me leverage my time and energy. It still wasn't enough. I was always busier than I *truly* wanted. But I thought that this was part of doing business. It's what I saw all around me. I didn't see *anyone* being 100 percent happy with their business or life or lifestyle. In fact, my business and lifestyle were more ideal than that of *anyone* I knew!

So I accepted this cycle as part of business and part of life. I didn't think there was anything I could do about it. I managed my energy and enjoyed my business as best I could. After all, how lucky was I to even have a business and life that were 90 percent ideal? I already had it so much better than most people around me. Why want even more? Was it *really* even possible to have it all? I didn't think so. I focused on feeling grateful for doing work I loved and having more freedom and alone time than ever before. And that 10 percent that I missed? I accepted it as part of the deal. Doesn't everyone have to sacrifice *something* to grow their business? Doesn't everyone have to sacrifice *something* to receive *anything*? Everyone around me seemed to think so, and I didn't question it either.

Introvert Introspections:

- On a scale of 1 (not at all) to 10 (completely!), how ideal are your business and lifestyle right now?
- What would need to change to get to a 10?
- Do you believe it's possible to create a business and life that are 100 percent ideal for you?
- If not, what do you think you need to sacrifice or change to grow your business and realize your dreams?

Chapter 5

Sick and Tired of Coaching

In 2008, I fulfilled the two biggest dreams I had since I started my business: My business was doing well, and I published my first book.

I could have continued on the path I was on. But doing the same things over and over doesn't make me happy. I always want to learn, grow, and create something new. So I asked myself: what's next?

The answer came up instantly and excited me deeply. It also scared me to death: to reach millions of women all over the globe with my message and work.

WHAT?!! Hell no! That dream sounded too big and too scary, not to mention completely impossible.

I mean, I worked as a coach in The Netherlands, in Dutch only. I had NO desire to travel the world or to be around people all the time. How could I possibly reach millions of people? Without getting busier and having even less alone time?

That vision seemed too big and the price (less alone time and less freedom!) felt too high. So I buried this dream. DEEP. I focused on learning to work online and creating online group programs to leverage my time and create more space in my schedule.

The dream resurfaced now and then, but I successfully suppressed it for a while, until 2010 when I realized I was DONE coaching people. I no longer wanted to coach people to find their purpose, and I no longer wanted to work with employees. I couldn't stand it anymore!

I turned my knowledge into an online program and sold it one last time. The money I made with this program allowed me to take a short sabbatical to figure out what I wanted to do next. I had *no* clue if I still wanted to be a coach or if I'd do something completely different. I didn't care.

I followed my intuition, and after a couple of months, my next mission was clear: to work globally, with women entrepreneurs.[*]

In November 2011, I wrote my first English newsletter. In December, I launched a brand-new online program for my brand-new audience. It sold out within two weeks, and I was super happy about that!

By January 2012, I was off to a great and adventurous start. I hired a business coach for a year and couldn't wait to get my new business off the ground!

Introvert Introspections:

- What (and perhaps who) are you completely DONE with in your business?
- What would you love instead?
- What's next for YOU?

---

[*] If you want to know how I got clear on my new dream, check out my book *Unmute Your Life - break free from fear and go for what you REALLY want.* In it, I describe how I figured out my new mission. You can read all about the book here: www.unmuteyourlife.com

Chapter 6

The Birth of the Happy Hermit

During 2012, I spoke regularly with my business coach. We talked about my plans and actions, my mindset and energy. Every time something triggered a feeling of busyness or overwhelm, I hit the brakes on our conversation. I knew this feeling too well! It was the contracted feeling I always suffered from when I had too little alone time and not enough down time in my schedule.

Every time I noticed this feeling of restriction, I said to my coach: "Wait a minute. This isn't right. My inner hermit isn't happy, so something needs to change." Then we'd tweak things until my inner hermit calmed down. (I came up with the term "inner hermit" because it succinctly described what needed our attention: the part of me that was worried I wouldn't have enough solitude, space, and freedom.) I rescheduled appointments, took on fewer projects, postponed launches, or made other changes that made me feel freer.

Everything went well. My business grew, private clients showed up out of nowhere, and I was happy with the success of my new business.

In November, my coach and I went over my goals and plans for 2013. During that conversation, my inner hermit was restless. The plans sounded exciting but also overwhelming, busy, and complicated. (I like to keep things as simple as possible.) I sensed my plans didn't give me enough space or alone time.

My business was still 90 percent ideal for me. I still had more free time than most people around me. I was grateful that my new business was a success. And yet … it just wasn't enough. I started my business to feel free and do *everything* in my own way, *exactly* as I wanted to. I didn't start it to feel 90 percent free. I started it to experience 100 percent freedom!

As we continued to talk about my plans for 2013, my inner hermit became ever more restless, until the pressure became too much and I said: "NO. I'm not doing this anymore. I'm DONE being a crappy hermit. I'm going to be a happy hermit instead!"

Introvert Introspections:

- If you gave yourself permission to want even more than you already have, what would you want?
- If you gave yourself permission to be and feel 100 percent free, what would change? What would you do or stop doing?

Chapter 7

No More than Four Appointments per Week

It felt good to say it out loud: "I'm done being a crappy hermit. I'm going to be a happy hermit now!" The moment I said it, I could feel this decision in my bones. I was serious about *never* wanting to feel busy and drained again. I was grateful for the amount of space and freedom my business already gave me, *and* I wanted more. It was *my* business. *I* called the shots, and I decided to STOP settling for anything less than a business that was 100 percent ideal for me. Not 90 percent. Not 95 percent. Not even 99 percent. I wanted it all! I had *no* idea how to do it. But I made my decision, and I was not backing down.

"Okay," my coach said. "That's very clear, so let's look at the next step. How many appointments would you ideally like to make?" I didn't know, so we decided to talk about that on our next call.

I took out my new calendar for 2013 and stared at the empty pages. I imagined what it would look like if the pages were filled with appointments, and how that made me feel.

First, I imagined what ten appointments per week would feel like. AAAHHHHH!!!!!! That caused an instant stomach cramp. No way! That was too much!

I dropped to eight appointments and still felt squeezed. Apparently, eight appointments were still too many.

Then I imagined what it would feel like to only make six appointments per week. Ah! That felt good! The knot in my stomach dissolved. I could breathe again and felt my body relax. Six appointments it was!

I felt relieved. But the first doubt showed up, too. Only six appointments? How was that even possible? It felt good, though, so I figured I'd found my ideal number of appointments.

Two weeks later, I talked to my coach again. She asked me if I came up with a number of appointments that felt good to me. "I did!" I said, "Six appointments per week sounds ideal!"

"Are you sure?" she asked. The answer immediately came up. No. I wasn't sure. Six appointments were still too much.

I took a moment to get quiet, turn inward, and explore some more. How did five appointments feel? Hm … better! But not completely free yet. I dropped to four appointments and felt *immense* relief. This was good. It felt free and spacious! I had my answer. I wanted only four appointments per week. That was the absolute maximum!

Introvert Introspection:

- What's your ideal number of appointments per week? Or, what's your ideal number of working hours per week? Or, what's your ideal number of projects you like working on simultaneously?

Don't think about what's possible or how to make it work. For now, just dream. What would give you the most perfect sense of freedom and space? What feels absolutely ideal for you?

Chapter 8

The Next Steps

Two things were clear: I was going to be a happy hermit, and I'd make a maximum of four appointments per week. I was committed to doing whatever it took to make this a reality. Mind you, I had NO idea what it would take. I didn't know how I could grow my business while making so few appointments. I didn't even know if it was possible at all! But I was determined. And I knew that whatever I set my mind to is what I would get. I didn't know *how* I could become a happy hermit, but I was certain that I would!

It's important to pay attention to this part for your own journey, so I'll repeat the key ideas I want you to remember:

- I didn't know HOW I could achieve my goal.
- I didn't even know if it was possible at all! But I went for it anyway.

Most people drop their dream when they realize they don't know *how* to get what they want. They mistakenly think that they need to know *how* they can accomplish something, or else they can't achieve it. They also think they need to believe something is possible before they can manifest it.

Both assumptions aren't true. You don't have to know how you can realize your dream, and you don't have to be doubt-free either. The only things you need are:

- A clear decision. Choose what you want and say "YES" to it.
- Commitment. Be committed to doing what it takes to realize your dream. Even when you're not sure if it's possible to achieve it, you can still be all in! After all, you can't be certain what's possible until you go for your goal.
- An open mind. Become curious about what might be possible and how good it can get!

After I knew what I wanted and decided to achieve it, the next step was to act on my decision to limit my appointments to a maximum of four per week. So that's where I started. It simply looked like this: I didn't make more than four appointments per week. My appointments are usually one hour, which means I had a maximum of four hours of *direct* interaction per week. These are my *business* appointments. I don't include the time I spend on social media and answering emails or audio messages from my private clients. Since that doesn't require direct interaction and I can respond whenever it feels inspired, it doesn't drain me.

These four hours do NOT include lunch or dinner dates with family or friends. I can tell you how often I plan those: two maximum per week. (But that rarely happens. It's usually one per week, and definitely not every week.) I talk to friends or my parents on the phone now and then. This is also NOT included in my weekly appointments.

I was super strict about my maximum number of appointments and didn't make ANY exceptions. When you're not strict, you'll *never* create a schedule that's ideal for you. Making exceptions will become your default state. That's not what I wanted.

I became even pickier about the appointments I made. I asked myself these questions for every appointment I made:

- Is it absolutely necessary to connect?
- Is this meeting an enrichment of my life?
- Does it sound like fun? If the answer was "no," I said, "no."

I was very intentional and never said "yes" (or "no") without thoroughly feeling it through. Yes, *feeling* it through. Your rational mind is not the right tool to determine which appointments to make. Your mind often brings up doubts and fears, urging you to make exceptions to your own rules.

Thankfully, I had already mastered setting boundaries and saying no.* I only had to practice asking myself what I *truly* wanted before I made an appointment.

I also made practical changes in my business. Changes that made it possible to grow my business and inspire more people without adding more work or appointments to my schedule. I share the changes I made in the next chapter.

The practical changes are the easy part of creating your ideal business and schedule, though. It's the *inner* part, your beliefs, doubts and fears, that are difficult to change. When you're clear on the inside, the outer actions fall easily into place. I share the inner shifts I needed to make in Chapter 10, *The Hardest Part of Making My Business Ideal for Me*.

But first, let's look at the practical changes I made so I could grow my business, while creating more space, time, and freedom at the same time.

---

* If you want to learn how to say no and set boundaries (and prioritize yourself, your dreams, and your well-being), my book *The Art of Divine Selfishness - transform your life, your business & the world by putting YOU first* is just what you need: www.divinelyselfish.com

Introvert Introspections:

- What does your ideal schedule look like?
- How many appointments would you ideally like to make per week? (Minimum and maximum. I don't have a minimum, by the way. I'm okay with zero appointments per week!) Check the answer you gave in the previous chapter. Is that *really* your ideal number of appointments, projects, or hours? Are you sure?
- What are your criteria for the appointments you make or the projects you accept? What determines if you say "yes" or "no"?

You can sign up for a free Ideal Schedule Worksheet that helps you create your perfect schedule at www.bookfreebees.com

Chapter 9

Practical Changes

These are the practical changes I made to create more time and space in my schedule.

Number of private clients and fees

Since the beginning of my business, I've always limited the number of private clients I worked with simultaneously to eight. But I often made exceptions to that rule. Because I really liked the person and was eager to work with them. Or because I feared I'd lose the client if I put them on a waiting list.

I stopped making exceptions and stuck to my maximum of eight private clients. I also raised my private coaching fees.

Over the years, I've changed the maximum amount of private clients I work with at the same time. It's seven people now, unless I feel I want more space and (temporarily) lower the number to five.

Online programs / group programs

I started creating group programs in 2006. Working with groups was a great way to leverage my time. But it still took up large chunks of time AND required a lot of direct interaction. (A three-hour, in-person workshop equals three hours of being around people. That's super draining for me.) My first group programs still demanded a lot of time and direct interaction. I used to include group calls, Q&A calls, and private coaching calls for each participant, too.

Because the in-person workshops were so demanding, in 2008, I started creating online group programs. I could now serve more people while never leaving my house. Hermit heaven! I gradually moved *all* my work online, including my private coaching. It saves time and is much less draining.

Now, I offer my new, online programs only once live. Most programs have one or two group Q&A calls, and I pre-record most classes. I also include an online forum where people can ask me questions. I'm available to support my clients without having direct interaction with them.

After I offer an online program live, including support, once, it becomes an evergreen product. People can purchase and access the content, but it no longer includes access to me (so it doesn't cost me any time).

Outsourcing / delegating

I started outsourcing work for a couple of hours per month around 2008. It felt soooo scary at the time! I wasn't sure I'd make enough money to pay my virtual assistant each month. It also felt scary to let go of control.

I quickly got used to it, though, and delegated more and more work over the years. One thing I was thrilled to hand over to my team was answering my emails. Not those of my private clients—they have direct access to me and can email me as often as they like. All other emails go directly to my team. These are, for example, emails with questions about invoices or downloading materials, inquiries for interviews, or questions about my services or coaching.

Phone

No one has my phone number. I have a landline in case I need to give my phone number (sometimes it's a requirement). If someone calls, they get my voicemail. (Which tells you I rarely listen to these messages, and it's best to reach me via email.) I have a mobile phone, but only a handful or friends and family members have that number. Like most introverts, I hate the intrusion of being called, so my phone is always on mute. :-)

Introvert Introspections:

- How could you leverage your time better?
- What could free up space and time for you?

Chapter 10

The Hardest Changes to Make

The hardest part of creating my ideal business wasn't the practical actions I took. The practical aspect of anything is *never* the hardest part! It's always the inner part that's most difficult: the doubts, fears, and limiting beliefs that show up once you decide to make a change.

My decision to become a happy hermit triggered A LOT of insecurities and doubts. None of them were new. I'd addressed them before, but apparently, they weren't completely gone yet. That's usually the case. Healing and transformation often happen in layers. Every time you address an issue or fear, a part of it gets healed. The next time you encounter the same fear or limiting belief, you heal a deeper layer of it. And so on, until it's completely cleared. If you recognize the same fears come up in new situations, know that this is common!

My fears didn't stop me. My fears simply showed me I had more inner work to do. Which I happily did! The reward—a business that's 100 percent ideal for me and ALL the freedom and alone time I craved since I was a kid (seriously!)—was MORE than worth it!

Here are the fears and doubts that came up for me. Perhaps you recognize one or more of them.

Fear: I felt ashamed

This was a BIG one. How could I love people, yet couldn't stand them when I overdosed on human contact? More importantly, how could I work as a coach yet only enjoy a *very* minimal dose of human interaction? When I looked at fellow coaches, NO ONE got "peopled out" as quickly as I did (or at all!). They made appointments back-to-back, day in, day out, and seemed to love that. It made me doubt if there was something wrong with me.

Reality: there was never anything wrong with me

I had internalized messages I received from a very young age that gave me the impression that I needed to be different. Most of us receive messages like that. And the same is true for you: there was never anything wrong with you. You are who you are because that is exactly who you're meant to be. The universe doesn't make mistakes. Everyone is born exactly as they're supposed to be.

Fear: I worried if I'd be able to make enough money

Would it *really* be possible to make enough money while I increased my freedom? Would it *really* be possible to grow my income if I worked with *fewer* clients?

Reality: money and action aren't necessarily related

Most of us learn that you can only make money when you *work* for it. Making money requires action! As a result, you automatically believe the opposite as well: *not* working equals *not* making money. So, when it's your work to work with people, and you work with fewer people, it makes sense that your income goes down, doesn't it?

Wrong.

First, this is wrong from a practical standpoint. When you raise your fees, you can work with fewer people and still make more money. When you create other streams of income, you can work less and make more.

Second, this is wrong from an energetic standpoint. Money, like everything else, is energy. The source of money (the source of *everything*) is Source itself. The universe, god, goddess, All-That-Is, The Field—call it what you want, THAT'S the source of EVERYTHING. The universe is the source and the creator of *everything that exists*. And you create everything from the inside out, from the consciousness that you are. It all starts inside of YOU. Everything you create (and you create *everything* in your life) is a co-creation between you and the universe. Your *energy* and consciousness determine your results, *not* your actions.

This energetic standpoint may or may not speak to you. If not, ignore it and only remember the first one: there are endless ways to receive money besides actually *working* for it. Think about things like investing, for example. That's another way to make money that's not directly related to taking daily action.

Fear: I worried if my clients would accept my decision

Would people want to work with a coach who only wants to be around people for a limited amount of time? Or would they think I hated people and wouldn't feel comfortable hiring me? What if I lost ALL my clients?! That would be the end of my business! I'd have to go back to a job and lose all my freedom! OMG. That was the *last* thing I wanted!

*Reality: people want to work with me BECAUSE
I'm different from most other coaches*

Many of my clients are introverts, too, and they're eager to make their businesses introvert friendly. A lot of my clients are extroverts, though. They're excited about doing business in their own way, too.

What all of my clients have in common is that they've always felt different. Because the work they do is revolutionary; because they're changemakers who question or disrupt the status quo; because they're creative and spiritual and never felt like they fitted in; and because "normal" ways of doing business don't work for them. They crave to do business in their own way, on their own terms. Seeing me do that in ways that are definitely NOT the norm inspires them. It shows them it's possible for *them* to be completely true to themselves in their business and life, too!

Introvert Introspections:

- What do you fear about making your business completely ideal for you?
- What do you doubt you'll be able to change? Do you think you can lower your number of projects, clients, appointments, or working hours and still make enough (or even more!) money, for example? Do you think you'll be able to take more time off? Do you think you can get to a place where you love everything about your business? Do you believe that you can be true to yourself in your marketing?
- Ask yourself for each fear or doubt you write down: Are you 100 percent certain this is true? Or might something else be true, too?

Part Four of the book takes you through common fears that can come up when you change your business. Chances are your fears are addressed there.

Chapter 11

The First Year

The first quarter wasn't easy. My income plummeted. I stopped taking on new coaching clients to make space in my schedule, but I didn't have online programs for my new business yet. (I no longer delivered the online program I had created before. The way I set that up cost me too much time and energy.) This caused some financial stress.

I also had to make practical changes that took extra money, time, and energy. I delegated more (which cost more), I hired a new coach (which also cost more), and I created a new online program for my new business (which also cost me time, energy, and money).

It felt weird and highly uncomfortable to finally have the freedom I had craved since I was a child. As I mentioned before, the practical actions were easy. It was the inner work that was often hard: dealing with financial stress, and facing the fears and doubts I described in the previous chapter.

I was also detoxing from beliefs that made it hard to enjoy my newfound freedom. Like most people, I was conditioned to believe that in order to achieve something, you need to *do* something. If you want to achieve more, you need to *do* more. You need to use your time wisely and productively. You can't be lazy! You can't expect to grow your business while you're pottering around without doing much of anything! Those, and other beliefs around work, money, and manifestation came up daily. I felt like I did something wrong every day. Shouldn't I be DOING more? Shouldn't I be more productive now that I had more time? Was I *really* doing the right things? When your income drops, surely that's a sign that you're doing something wrong?

Thankfully, I had a truckload of mindset and energy shifting tools at my disposal that I could use to transform my beliefs and let go of my fears and doubts.

It took me a while to get used to my freedom and thoroughly shift my beliefs. I see this in my clients, too. It's one thing to know what your ideal business and lifestyle look like. It's another to realize it. You'll encounter *every* single belief, fear, and doubt that stands between you and your desired reality. It's important to know this upfront so you don't back down when your fears appear. This is normal, and you have what it takes to move through it!

My fears and doubts came up the moment I decided to become a happy hermit. I made sure I wouldn't go back on my decision by writing a blog about it. I published *My personal story—a message from the cave** on November 23, 2012. I was nervous. How would people respond? Would I lose clients? It was scary, but I felt I had to do it. Announcing publicly that I was making drastic changes helped me to stay committed to my decision. It also felt right to take a stand for my truth and my happiness.

Turns out, I didn't lose any clients. This blog brought in more clients! My story inspired people, and they recognized themselves in it. I had no idea before I posted that blog!

Getting positive feedback helped me stay on track. But even if I'd been criticized, I'd have stayed true to my decision. I was determined to *finally* create ALL the freedom and space I chose for myself, and nothing and no one was going to stop me!

After the first quarter of 2013, I'd found my footing. I made the practical changes I needed to make; my new online program was about to be launched; I had my ideal amount of private clients; *and* I

---

* You can read this blog post at the end of this book.

was getting used to having a massive amount of alone time, freedom, and space. I LOVED it! It was an immense relief to finally feel *happy* about being super introverted, instead of resisting it. The *joy* I felt when I looked at my calendar and saw almost empty page after page after page … I loved that more than words can express. (I still do!)

Introvert Introspections:

- What change(s) would you like to make in your business and / or lifestyle?
- How can you hold yourself to that decision and support your commitment? (For example, by writing a blog about it / hiring a coach / asking someone to hold you accountable / or another way?)

Chapter 12

How It Is Now, Eight Years Later

After that rocky first quarter, my new happy hermit lifestyle was a given. I never looked back!

Over the years, I created more online programs. I continued to work with only a handful of private clients. Occasionally I made an exception on my maximum of four appointments per week, but I can count the number of times that happened on two hands.

In January 2017, I added something new: a monthly hermit week—a completely appointment-free week. The idea came to me when I bought my new diary. I looked at the empty pages and wondered what it would feel like to have *zero* appointments in a week now and then. That idea instantly felt fantastic! I decided to give myself these hermit weeks and see how that would be. The first thing I put in that new diary were all the hermit weeks of the year. :-)

I loved these weeks from the start and honor them to this day. My hermit weeks are still the first thing I put in my new diary each year!

I might make more changes to my schedule in the future. You never know! For now, the way I run my business, what I do, and how I do it is absolutely ideal for me. The moment this changes, I'll make tweaks so that my business always serves ME, instead of the other way around.

> *Introvert Introspections:*
>
> - Does your business serve you, or do you serve your business?
> - What would it feel and look like if your business served you completely?

PART TWO

Your Journey

Mindset and Inner Foundation

Introduction

In Part Two, I take you through the qualities, strengths, and habits that help you create a thriving business—on your terms.

Your inner world (everything you think, feel, and believe) is the foundation for the realization of your dreams. When your inner world is in order, the outer manifestation can fall into place. The following chapters help you create a strong inner foundation so you and your business can thrive!

You can read the chapters in any order you like. **Just read the following chapter,** *It's a Step-by-Step Process,* **first.** That chapter helps take away any dread or overwhelm you may feel about changing your business and life.

Chapter 1

It's a Step-by-Step Process (and Easier than You Think!)

Maybe you're excited to change your business. But maybe you feel overwhelmed by everything you think you must do.

Let me put your mind at ease. Creating a business and life you adore is a *process*. It's a series of *daily* decisions and actions that, over time, result in a business and life you're in love with. You don't even have to know your dream in detail or how to realize it, because creating your ideal business comes down to this: making choices and taking actions daily that feel like the right thing to do (even when they scare you or make you feel uncomfortable).

The life and business I have today I couldn't have realized in one day, not even in one year! It began with an ongoing series of actions and decisions that started a long, *long* time ago. The first action step was hiring a career coach to help me figure out what meaningful and fulfilling work looked like for me. Since then, I have continued to focus on what I *truly* want. I am where I am today because I always explore what I *really* want and take actions that are aligned with my desires.

Creating a business and life you love is a journey. You won't accomplish it overnight, but don't let that scare you off! Once you start making daily choices based on what you *truly* want—from what to have for dinner to speaking your mind to declining an invitation to a party—YOUR LIFE IMPROVES GINORMOUSLY. **Your ideal schedule and the business and life of your dreams will fall into place because of your daily choices and actions.**

Ask yourself the following questions* to make daily decisions that bring you closer to your dreams. You don't have to answer each question separately. Just read through them and notice what thoughts or emotions come up. Or pick one question and use it as a journal prompt. Write it in your journal and, for ten minutes, write down *everything* that comes up.

- What feels right for you today?
- What would bring you joy today?
- What do you *know* deep down matters most today?
- What, if any, decision do you need to make?
- What, if any, action do you need to take based on what your gut tells you?
- Who (and how) do you need to be today to bring what you *truly* want closer to you?
- What guidance does your intuition / your soul have for you today?
- Does this support the business and life you love? If not, what does? (Ask this question before you take an action or make a decision.)

Continue to ask yourself these questions, and *act* on the answers you get. You'll immediately feel happier and more fulfilled. Your business and life will start morphing into their most ideal form for you, starting today!

It's okay to take baby steps. It's okay to take your time. It's okay to be true to your own pace, no matter how "slow" or "quick" that seems

---

* I put these questions on a beautiful PDF you can print, so it's easy to use them regularly. You can sign up for this PDF and other bonus gifts at www. bookfreebees.com

to be. It's okay to make mistakes, and it's okay to change your mind. Just follow what feels right for you each day, and your ideal business and life will fall into place.

Introvert Introspections:

- What's ONE decision you can make now that will bring your ideal business and life closer to you?
- What (small) step can you take based on that decision?

Chapter 2

Decide

Everything you create, every goal you achieve, every dream you realize, begins with a decision.

Most people have it backward. They think they need to know *how* they can achieve something before they decide to go for it. If they can't see the path toward their goal, they often stop before they start. But that's not how realizing goals works, *especially* goals that seem unattainable or scary.

I didn't *know* how I could realize my ideal lifestyle. I wasn't even certain that it was possible to make fewer appointments, create more space, and still grow my business. But I didn't let that stop me. I decided it would happen somehow, and let the universe figure out the details. Because *that's* how manifestation works: *you* decide what you want. *The universe* figures out the logistics and brings you the inspiration for the actions, decisions, or changes you need to make. You receive this guidance through your intuition and knowing it deep down. Then, it's *your job* to act on the guidance you receive. That is the essence of manifestation and reaching all goals. **And this chain of creation starts with your decision.**

Until you say "yes" to your dream, you actually say "no" to it. Nothing moves, nothing flows, nothing happens until you say "YES!"

Saying "yes" opens the door to your intuition, ideas, inspiration, and synchronicities. Your eyes are open to possibilities and options you couldn't see before.

You don't have to know *how* you can create your ideal business and lifestyle. The steps will reveal themselves along the way. But until you decide, nothing happens.

You may need to say "yes" to your dream more than once, especially when your dream feels scary. Sometimes even daily! That's not unusual. Nothing is wrong and you're not doing anything wrong.

Introvert Introspections:

- Are you ready to say "YES!" to your ideal business and lifestyle (even if you're not sure what it looks like yet)?
- If not, how could you feel more ready soon? (Is there something you can do? Someone who can help? A book you can read, a coach you can hire, a friend you can talk to?)

Chapter 3

Be Willing

Be willing to face uncertainty, especially when your ideal business looks different from other businesses. Be willing to feel uncomfortable. Be willing to face your fears and doubts. Be willing to change, to grow, to face your resistance, to expand, and to do things differently. Be willing to let go of what you know and enter uncharted territory. All you have to do is say this:

Yes, I am willing to do what it takes to see my dreams come to life!

> *Introvert Introspection:*
>
> - Are you willing to do what it takes to realize your dream, even if you don't know what it will take yet?

(If your answer is *no*, you haven't landed on your *true* dream yet—or you haven't let yourself feel how much you want it. When you connect to *why* you want something and how it will feel to have it in your life, your dream becomes bigger and more powerful than your fears. This will help you say "yes" to your dream and commit to doing what it takes to let it unfold.)

Chapter 4

Take a Stand for Who You Are

When you create a business that's ideal for you, you build your business around *yourself*. Not around your clients and their demands. Not around a gap in the market. You don't base the way you do business on what others do. You shape your entire business around your soul, personality, dreams, wants, and needs. This is the best way to make sure your business and life are ideal for *you*. But you need to accept *every* part of who you are first. You need to take a stand for who you are and what you want.

As I wrote before, I used to feel weird about needing so much alone time. As long as I felt ashamed about that, it was impossible to create the lifestyle and business I have today. I had to make peace with my introversion and other aspects of myself *first*. Like my love for a simple, quiet life. I didn't know how that matched with my mission to reach millions of women around the globe. Or my desire for lots of time to just putter around. How lazy is that?! Now, I love that about myself. But a couple of years ago, I still bought into the productivity myth that told me I needed to spend my time wisely and productively and not piss it away, staring out the window, watching a series, or just doing nothing *while there were so many "useful" things I could do instead!*

If I hadn't fully accepted those aspects of myself, I'd still be a crappy hermit today. I'd still long for more quiet and inner peace without finding it. I'd still be on the rollercoaster of either having enough money *or* having enough alone time. And I could *never* have written this book if I hadn't fully accepted my inner hermit!

It's impossible to build your business around yourself if you don't fully accept yourself first. This begins with giving yourself permission to be the person you are born to be. Then you can accept who you are and *own* (and even love) everything that makes you *you*.

Many people don't accept themselves completely. They think they should hide certain parts of themselves, especially in their business. But I've learned that the opposite is true. You don't have to change who you are to grow your business and create a business and life you adore. On the contrary! All you have to do is become even MORE of who you already are. Being unapologetically true to yourself is the foundation of thriving, happy business and life!

Introvert Introspections:

- What part(s) of yourself don't you fully accept yet?
- What would change in your business and life when you accepted this part?

Chapter 5

Take a Stand for What You Want

Be bold. Be clear. Know what you want, and *own* it. Claim it. Take a stand for it. Don't water down your desires. Don't judge or criticize them. Don't justify them either. You don't have to explain why you want something—not even to yourself. Give yourself permission to want what you want and to receive it!

Don't worry about what others may think about you or your desires. Let them worry about their own dreams. *You* only have to focus on *your* dreams.

Feel. Explore. What is it you want? What is it you *REALLY* want? And why do you want it?

You don't have to know how (or if) you can accomplish it. Think about what you want and take a stand for it first. The "how" will fall into place after you decide to get what you want.

Remember: It's your business. It's your life. You're the boss. You can *do* and *desire* whatever you like. (As long as no one gets hurt, of course.)

Introvert Introspection:

- If you gave yourself permission to dream as big, bold, and / or "unrealistic" as you like, what would you dream of?

Chapter 6

Take a Stand for What You KNOW Deep Down

Deep down, you already know what's right for you. And you always know when something feels off. Take your inner nudges and niggles seriously. Don't dismiss them. They guide you on your path!

I knew for a long time that setting big, bold business goals and turning those into business or marketing plans was not for me, for example. No matter how hard I tried, I never stuck to my plans and rarely achieved my goals. Plans made me feel restricted and inflexible. Goals felt fun for a while, but they always led to stress and disappointment in the end. But all my business coaches told me I needed goals and a plan. Because you need direction. Because it propels you forward. Because you can't grow your business without setting goals and turning them into a solid business plan. So I tried, year after year, to set goals, make plans, and stick to them. I tried different ways of setting goals and making plans, but I still didn't stick to them. Yet I kept trying. Why? Because I took my business coaches' advice more seriously than I took my intuition. These coaches made more money than me and they reached more people. So clearly, I thought, they knew better than me.

They didn't. They knew what worked for THEM. And yes, setting goals and making plans works for many people. Perhaps for most people, even. I don't know and I don't care. The only thing I DO know is that it doesn't work for me. And I knew that since the day I started my business. I was overruling my "inner knowing" because I thought others knew better than I did.

I finally listened to what I already knew and stopped making plans and setting goals in 2016. I never looked back. Not setting goals or following plans feels good! Sometimes I make a rough outline of a plan for a project or a book launch, if it feels inspired. I make action lists every week. I love making lists. And I love ticking items off of it even more. Tick! That's it. In addition to lists, I go with what my soul guides me to do. It works like a charm for me!

When you do what feels right for *you*, that's *always* the way that works *best* for you. Even if no one else does it that way. Even when it works for nobody else. Even when so-called "experts" tell you to do something a certain way, or else you can't get what you want. Ignore them. Listen to what you KNOW deep down, and trust that more than *anything* and *anyone* else.

Introvert Introspections:

- If you listened to what you know deep down and / or feel called to do, what would change?
- What would you do?
- What would you stop doing? What would be different?

Chapter 7

Courage

Building your business around your personality and ideal lifestyle takes courage. Courage to do things differently and forge your own path. The courage to take risks and step into the unknown.

If you can use some bravery now, I'd like to remind you that you already have that in spades. You do! For starters, you're an entrepreneur. Starting a business takes guts! You dared to do a lot of other things in your life, too. Over the years, you took many risks and stepped into the unknown more often than you can remember, so tell yourself that you can continue to take risks and steps into the unknown because you've done it before!

If you feel scared, remember to shift your perspective. Stop looking at what might go wrong and look at what could go right. Stop looking at what you might lose and focus on what you can gain instead. Plus, it's always better to give your dreams a try than to regret never giving them a chance.

Introvert Introspections:

- What have you dared in your life before? What scared the crap out of you once that worked out great for you?

Think all the way back to your childhood. Make a list. Write *everything* down from learning to ride a bike to giving a speech. Seeing how courageous you've been throughout your life helps you take bolder steps now.

Chapter 8

Choose to Trust

Choose to trust yourself. Choose to trust that you'll be fine. Choose to trust that you'll always know what to do.

I wasn't sure if I could make my ideal lifestyle work AND still grow my business. I didn't know if it was possible. But I trusted that I'd find my way. That's what I *chose* to trust. Looking back at my life, I could see that everything always worked out for me in the end. Even the most difficult situations had resolved in beneficial ways. Sometimes it happened because of something I did, sometimes it happened due to something magical and unexplainable, and sometimes it happened due to a combination of my own actions and cosmic intervention. I remember applying for a job and not getting it, for example. I was so disappointed—until I found a *much* better job, closer to home, a couple of weeks later. I also felt devastated when a seven-year long relationship ended when I was in my twenties. All I can say now is, thank *god* that relationship ended when it did! I learned a lot from that relationship and I'm grateful for the experience, but I'm even more grateful that it ended and I found a new partner who is *so much* better for me.

What seems like a setback or terrible experience at the time can turn out to be a blessing later. That's not always clear when you're in the middle of it, though. I like to remind myself of the phrase *rejection is god's protection* in those moments, to remind myself that something better is on its way to me—even when I can't see it yet.

When you look back, can you see how everything always worked out for you in the end? Can you remember situations that seemed like a total disaster that turned out to be blessings in disguise?

To trust is a choice you make. *Choose* to trust that there is *always* a way to do business your way. You may not see how it's possible now, but you can choose to trust that it will fall into place somehow. Hasn't it always?

Introvert Introspections:

- Look back at your life, and write down five to ten examples that prove that you can trust yourself. Remember the times you did the right thing; you knew what to do; you made the right decision, and you trusted your intuition.
- Think about situations that seemed bad at the time but turned out to be blessings in disguise. Like a partner leaving and you ending up with a much better relationship with someone else. Or not getting hired and finding a much better job the next month. We all have experiences like these in our lives. Remember them and see how things have worked out for you in the past. Doesn't it make sense that this will *also* be the case now and in the future?

Chapter 9

Be True to YOURSELF in Everything You Do

Make it a habit to always ask yourself what *you* want. What feels right to you? What feels true to you? What do you *truly* want? What would you do if you trusted that everything always works out for you and you feared nothing?

Ask yourself these questions regularly. Use them to make your decisions, from deciding if you'll accept an invitation to a party to determining the price of your new product. What feels best, true, and right to you? Stick to that, regardless of what others do or expect from you.

You know yourself best. And if you want to build a business and life you adore, you need to base your decisions on what *you* want. It's truly that simple.

If you don't want something, take it seriously. If you want something, take it seriously. When something feels wrong, don't assume there's something wrong with *you*. Assume there's something wrong, *period.* When something feels right, don't worry what others will think of it, if this is normal, or if this is how things are supposed to be done. **Assume that whatever feels right is right for you.** Be faithful to yourself and to what you know, want, need, and feel.

> *Introvert Introspections:*
>
> - If you were true to yourself in every aspect of your business and life, what would be different?
> - What would you do?
> - What would you let go of?

Chapter 10

Yes and No

Here's another simple guideline to create a business and life you love: say "yes" to everything you love, say "no" to everything else.

I know what you might be thinking. "But Brigitte, it's not that simple! There are things that must be done, whether or not I love them. I can't just say "no" to them! That's impossible!"

No, it's not.

Yes, there are things you need to do that you may not love. Here's what you can do about them.

First, check if this needs to be done at all. Does it? REALLY? If the honest answer is yes, ask yourself if *you* should be the one doing it. Is that so? REALLY? For example: I don't enjoy doing my admin tasks. Yet I have to if I don't want trouble with the tax authorities. So I do my admin and pay my taxes. But my bookkeeper does most of the work, so I don't have to do that boring stuff myself.

If there's something that needs to be done and it *has* to be done by you, you can change your attitude toward it. Perhaps you can make it fun (or at least less awful). If that's not possible, you can stop resisting it and accept that this is something you choose to do. That saves you a lot of energy! I stopped resisting going to the dentist, for example. I go because I choose to keep my teeth as healthy as possible, and I no longer resist these appointments. This saves me more energy than you can imagine! *At least* a week in advance I would start to dread having to go to the dentist, which was a total waste of my time and energy. Now that I've stopped resisting it (yes, dreading something is a form of resistance!), I can use that time and energy for better things, like writing. ;-)

Do what you love. Don't do what you don't love; delegate or outsource it. If you can't ditch, delegate, or outsource something, stop fighting it.

Introvert Introspections:

- Make a list of all the things you love to do. Go over each item.
- Do you spend enough time on each of them?
- If not, how could you do more of it?
- Make a list of all the things you don't love. Go over each item.
- Is there something you can change to make you love this (or at least dislike it less)?
- If not, are you 100 percent certain this needs to be done?
- If so, does it have to be done by you?
- If not, who could do it for you? (Now or in the future.)
- If you can't delegate it and the *only* one who can do it is you, are you willing to stop fighting and resisting it?

Even though my bookkeeper does most of my admin work, I still resisted the few things I had to do myself. As a result, I procrastinated on my admin tasks, and it took me forever because I disliked doing it so much. Since I decided to stop resisting my admin tasks and chose to see them as a *very* small price to pay for the freedom of having my own business, I no longer waste time procrastinating or hating doing my admin chores. This saves me a lot of time and hassle!

Chapter 11

You Are Worthy

Not feeling worthy to receive what you desire is something I see in a lot of my clients. I've definitely felt unworthy myself, too! I felt I had no right to more happiness or an even better life. I thought I had to somehow *earn* being worthy to receive what I wanted.

Until I realized that every human being is worthy, just because they *are*. You don't have to earn the right to breathe, the right to be, or the right to belong. *Everyone* is born worthy!

You're worthy to get what you want.

You're worthy to get what you need.

You're worthy to live the life of your dreams.

You're worthy to be endlessly happy.

You are worthy just because you are.

Introvert Introspection:

- If you truly believed you are worthy, what, if anything, would change for you?

Chapter 12

Take Charge

You're the boss of your business and life. You're the *creator* of your business and life. The only question is: are you creating consciously, based on what you desire? Or are you creating unconsciously, often based on avoidance and fear?

Get behind the steering wheel of your life. Know that *you* are the one creating your life, and *you* are the one who decides what your business looks like. Be decisive. Step into your role of boss because you ARE the boss. You're the boss of your life, your business, and yourself.

If you want to create a business and life you adore, you have to take charge. This doesn't mean you have to work hard or try to control or manage everything. It means that you're not passive, but decisive. You're not wishy-washy in what you want, but you confidently claim it.

Be bold and take risks. Life becomes so much better when you GO for your dreams and desires instead of only hope for things to change.

Introvert Introspections:

- Where are you being passive or waiting for others to decide your fate?
- What would it look like if you took charge in those areas?

Chapter 13

Intuition

You don't have to know how you can create the business and life of your dreams. All you have to do is know what you want and decide to get it. After that, it's up to your soul and the universe to show you the way. You don't have to figure that out. That's your soul's job. *Your* job is to follow the guidance your soul brings you. Your intuition, your body, and your feelings always tell you what that guidance is. Follow that as best you can as often as you can—preferably in each moment—and you'll always get what you need at the perfect time.

Your soul knows your desires and dreams, and knows *exactly* what you need to live a happy, fulfilled life. She guides you to receive everything you want and need via your intuition.

Pay attention to how you feel. Your feelings are an important guiding system. When something excites you and brings you joy, follow it! There's something there for you, if only a lot of joy.

Pay attention to the nudges and whispers of your intuition. You already know what that's like. Think back to when you followed your intuition. How did you know what to do? How did you recognize what your best action or decision was? Recognizing how your intuition spoke to you in the past helps you better recognize your intuition today.

Also pay attention to the things you just *know*, or your deep "inner knowing." Your inner wisdom never steers you wrong.

The best way to create a business that's completely ideal for you is to decide what you want and follow your intuition every step of the way. That's how you manifest and create *everything*, including a business that serves you and makes you happy.

Introvert Introspections:

- If you always listened to your intuition, what would be different?
- What's your intuition telling you now?

Chapter 14

Break the Rules
(or at Least Question Them)

There isn't just *one* way to succeed. There isn't just *one* way to grow your business. There isn't only *one* way to thrive. There are as many ways to grow your business and achieve your goals as there are people.

But that's not what we learn. We learn that there are certain steps you need to take to succeed. In business, for example, many people will agree that you need a website. You don't. You can find clients without an online presence. You also don't need a logo. You don't need a brand. You don't need to make videos and you don't need to have a podcast. As I wrote in a previous chapter, you also don't need to set goals or follow a business plan. These things *can* work—but they don't necessarily work for *you*.

I'm not saying *you* don't need a business plan, website, or big goals that excite you. If you enjoy making plans, setting goals, having a website, and making videos, go ahead!

What I'm saying is this: what works for millions of others won't automatically work for you, too. What others present as a rule that needs to be followed only tells you *one* thing: this rule is part of their mindset and beliefs. They believe *they* need it. That's it. That's ALL.

Question *everything* you think you "need" to do to grow your business and to thrive. If it doesn't feel right for you, something isn't right. Find out what feels off and adjust accordingly. Sometimes that means breaking a rule. Sometimes it means shifting your mindset. Whatever it means, the only one who knows what works for you is YOU.

Always remember that what works for others won't always necessarily work for you, too. What's true for others isn't automatically true for you either. Even if a certain strategy works for millions of others, this still doesn't mean that it'll work for you, too!

Use the strategies, tactics and "rules" that feel right for you. These will work for you. Ditch or break all other "rules." I'm not talking about breaking the law or acting in any way unethical or illegal. I'm talking about common ideas about growing a business. There's only one way for you, baby: YOUR way!

Introvert Introspections:

- What do you think you need to do to grow your business? Write down all your ideas and thoughts about this.
- For each item you wrote down, ask yourself: how does this make me feel? If it feels genuinely good, keep doing it. If something feels off, ask yourself:
- What exactly feels off? What, if anything, do I fear? What, if anything, do I resist? Why?
- Is there something you can tweak so that it feels good to you? If so, make the change and carry on. If not, ask yourself:
- What if I just stopped doing this? How does THAT feel?

See what comes up. Make adjustments where needed. Ditch the "rules" that don't feel good and aren't a good match for you. Then, back yourself. More on that in the next chapter.

Chapter 15

What You Believe In Is What Will Work for You

There are as many ways to grow your business as there are entrepreneurs. There's no one-size-fits all. There's no cookie-cutter recipe. There's only what works for *you*, and what doesn't. If a certain strategy or tool resonates with you, by all means, use it! But if it doesn't, then don't. Because the truth is this: **it's your *belief* in a structure, system or strategy that determines if it works for you, NOT the structure, system, or strategy itself!**

If you believe you can only grow your business when you post something on social media three times per day, you will have to do that to grow your business. If you believe you need a podcast to grow your business, you'll need a podcast to grow your business. NOT because you *need* a podcast, but because *you believe* it's a necessity. Your belief makes it so. When your beliefs and actions line up, whatever strategy you use will work for you. When your beliefs and actions aren't aligned, your results won't be as good.

This is something I struggled with for a while. A couple of years ago, I stopped making business plans and stopped setting any goals, as I wrote earlier. I decided what was best for me was to grow my business like I do everything else: by following my intuition and doing what feels right in each moment.

Back then, I believed that following my intuition was the best way to live my life. But I didn't fully believe yet that this was the best way to grow my business, too. Finding a parking spot or a bigger apartment by following my intuition? Sure. Grow my business that way? I wasn't convinced. A part of me still believed I had to work hard(er) to grow my business. Part of me believed I needed some sort of structure because I can't just wing it! Yet, I *was* winging it. I often felt guilty or weird about that. I questioned myself and my actions. Was I *really* doing the right things? Was it *really* possible to grow my business that way? Or should I just do what everyone else was doing? They seemed more successful than I was, so maybe I was doing something wrong.

Because my actions (going with the flow, working without a plan, doing what each moment calls for) didn't line up with my beliefs (part of me thought it was impossible to grow my business this way), my results weren't very good. Plus, it was tiring to constantly doubt myself.

Until I realized I had to back myself. I had to *decide* that *my* way was the *best* way for me. I had to *choose to believe* that I could achieve whatever I wanted by following my intuition. Including growing my business. Once I backed myself and my way of doing things, my results improved and I felt much more relaxed.

Make sure that what you *believe* is necessary to grow your business aligns with what you're actually *doing*. Choose how you want to grow your business. *Choose* how *you* believe this will work for you. Pay attention to how you achieve results in other areas of your business and life. Areas where you trust that you'll get what you want. What do you do in those stress-free areas? What do you believe? How do you act? How do you naturally approach things in your life?

Apply the way you naturally do things to the way you do business. *Choose* to believe this will bring you the results you want, and cast your doubts aside.

Remember: it's not the system, structure, or strategy that determines your results. It's your *belief* in what works for you that determines what works for you. **Every strategy works if you believe it will!**

Introvert Introspections:

- If you trusted that your way of naturally doing things is the best way to create a thriving business, what would change?
- What would you do?
- What would you stop doing?

Chapter 16

Future You

If you want to create something new, the first thing that needs to change is *you*. The person you are today brought you to where you are today. The person who realizes your new dreams is a different person. She believes different things. She acts different, feels different, and maybe even looks different.

Paint the picture of your future self, the evolved version of who you are today. Then *be* her *now*. You can do that by asking yourself each morning: what would future me do today? How would she handle this situation and what decision would she make? What would she let go of and what would she not worry about at all? Notice the answers that come up and act on them.

When I decided to become a happy hermit instead of a crappy hermit, I asked myself what the happy hermit looked like. Who was that future me? How did she feel? What did she think? The answers were clear. The happy hermit felt incredibly free. When she looked at her schedule, she felt happy. So much free space! She knew it was possible to make only four appointments per week and still grow her business. She trusted herself and her way of doing business. She believed that all she had to do to grow her business was to be completely true to herself in every area of her business and life. She always followed her intuition because she knew that was the best, easiest, and fastest path to receive everything she wanted.

That's what the happy hermit version of myself looked like back in 2012. I've long grown into that version of myself since. Now, there's a different next-level version of me, and I do my best to be her now.

There's always a new dream for you. Each new dream requires you to become a new and improved version of yourself. Most of the time, becoming your next-level self means to let go of anything that no longer serves you, to become even more true to yourself, and to express your true self even more.

Most people focus on what they think they have to *do* to realize their goals. But what you *do* isn't nearly as important as *who you need to be* to achieve your dream.

Paint the picture of your future self, the one who has already accomplished your dream. Once you know what she looks like, BE that version of you from now on. It will make a profound, positive difference for you!

Introvert Introspections:

- What does the future you, the one who already created a business and life you're madly in love with, look like?
- What does she believe?
- How does she feel?
- How does she act?
- What would she do today and how would she handle the actions you're about to take?

Chapter 17

The Most Important Questions to Ask

People commonly ask several questions when they think about their dreams. How can I do this? How can I achieve that? What do I need to *do* to make X happen?

These are NOT the right questions. As I mentioned before, the most important aspect of creating your ideal business and lifestyle is the *inner* aspect: your mindset, thoughts, fears, doubts, beliefs, and the stories you tell yourself. **When your inner world is in order, your desired outer reality will fall into place.** You may still need to take action, but those actions are simply practical steps.

What you need to do will become clear for you along the way. It will! Inspiration and ideas will come to you when you need them. The first and main thing to focus on is your inner world. Always. That's why "What do I need to do?" and "How can I achieve that?" aren't the right questions to ask. The most important questions you need to ask yourself are these.

- Who do I need to *be* to achieve this?
- What do I need to *heal* to let this unfold for me? (For example: past disappointments, experiences, shame, guilt, or pain you still carry with you.)
- What do I need to *let go of* to make this possible for me?

- What do I need to *believe* to create a business and life that are ideal for me?

These questions show you what needs to shift in your inner world. Once you make these inner shifts, the outer steps will become clear to you, and you'll be ready to take them.

I already described what I needed to heal, shift, and release to turn myself from a crappy hermit into a happy hermit. The most important shift for me was to accept and love myself unconditionally. I needed to let go of shame, of thinking that I wasn't good enough, of feeling guilty for wanting so much freedom and an amazing life.

What you need to release, heal, and let go of will be different from what I needed to shift. What you need to believe will be different, too. We each have our own beliefs, doubts, and fears that influence us. Just know this: you're capable of creating the life you would love to live. You're able to create a business that makes your heart sing. How do I know that? Because I've been coaching women since 2001 to help them create a life they adore, and I've seen them succeed over and over. And because I did it myself, and there's nothing special about me that isn't within your reach, too! We're all souls having a human experience, limitless beings with far greater power and possibilities than we give ourselves credit for.

Remember the questions I shared in this chapter. Make it a habit to ask them *before* you look at what you need to *do*. It doesn't matter what your goal or dream is. It doesn't matter if you dream of writing a book, opening a restaurant, growing your business, doubling your income, or losing weight. The first thing to look at is always: who do you need to be to allow this dream to unfold for you?

Introvert Introspections:

- Who do you need to be to create a business and life you adore?
- What do you need to believe, shift, heal, and / or let go of?

Chapter 18

What Do You Expect?

Be mindful of your expectations. What you expect to happen is what you put your focus on, consciously or unconsciously. What you put your focus on is where your energy flows. Where your energy flows is where your actions go. Your focus, energy, feelings, and actions combined determine what you will experience.

Expect you will create your ideal business. Expect that everything always works out for you. Expect you'll get the help and inspiration you need the moment you need it.

Expect to get what you want. Expect it will be easier than you think. Expect life to surprise and delight you!

Introvert Introspections:

- What do you expect from the process of creating your ideal business and life?

  If you're not sure what you expect, ask yourself what you think creating your ideal business and life will be like. Do you think it will be difficult / easy / impossible / a struggle / hard work / something else? *Every* answer is an expectation you have.

> • Look at each expectation. Does it make you feel good?
> Does it excite you? Does it uplift you? If not, change your
> expectation. Expect something better! You don't know
> what will happen, so you're guessing either way. Choose
> thoughts that make you feel better!

Often you can't go from "I think it will be difficult" to "I bet it will be super easy!" That might be too big of a jump. If that's the case, take a smaller step. Shift your mind from "I think it will be difficult" to "It might be easier than I think" or "I open myself up to the possibility that it could be easier than I think." Or shift your mind into general curiosity: "I wonder how this can unfold for me!"

Chapter 19

Choose How You Want to Feel

Sometimes you're not clear about what you want. No matter how long you think about it, you just don't know how many appointments you want to make per week. Or you don't know what you love to do most. Or what your ideal business and / or life look like.

That's okay. You don't have to know. The only thing you need to know is how you want to *feel*. What do you want to feel and experience more of? Freedom? Beauty? Joy? Space? Creativity? Love? Connection?

Whatever you want to feel more of, *feel* what it feels like in your body. Give your soul the instruction to bring you the ideas and experiences that will make you feel this way. Then follow your intuition and inner nudges.

Introvert Introspections:

- What do you want to feel or experience more of in your business? In your life?
- What could make you feel that way today?

PART THREE

Practical Tips to Make Your Business Introvert Friendly

Introduction

The following chapters take you through some general tips to make your business more introvert friendly. Notice what resonates with you. Write down the ideas that speak to you and implement them in your business, step by step.

If doubts come up, remind yourself that there's *always* a way to do business in *your* own way. There really is! If you believe in yourself and take a stand for what you want, you can do anything you choose. You're in charge, you're the boss, and you decide how to run your business (and life)!

Read through the chapters in any order you like, as long as you start with the first chapter. You must know how much alone time you want so you can create a schedule that gives you enough time for yourself. Introverts need alone time to recharge, so you need to build some solitude into your schedule. The balance between alone time and interaction with others is a key element to focus on to thrive as an introvert entrepreneur.

If you want to create a business and life you adore, you also need to know what your *true* dreams are. You need to know what makes your business and life meaningful and fulfilling. Book One in the Art of Divine Selfishness Series, *Unmute Your Life - break free from fear & go for what you REALLY want,* can help you get clarity.

Chapter 1

How Much Alone Time Do You Need?

Do you know how much alone time and how much interaction you need to feel energized and whole? Introverts need time alone to find energy, so it's important to create a business / lifestyle / schedule that allows you the solitude you crave. You may not be able to create your optimum amount of space *yet*, but at least you'll know what to aim for.

How do you know how much alone time you need? It starts with paying attention. Notice when you start to feel drained. Notice when you can't stand people anymore—that's a sure sign you need time for yourself. Notice when the thought of talking with someone feels like too much. These can all be signs you've had enough (or too much) human interaction. Pay attention to how you feel and check what made you feel that way. That's the best way to find out what you need. Here's how I know I've had an overload of interaction and human contact:

- Everything feels like it's too much.
- I feel drained.
- I'm cranky and quickly irritated.
- I want to be left alone.
- Even *thinking* about talking to or seeing people wears me out.

- I have even less tolerance for loud noises, or any sounds, really. (It needs to be quiet!)
- When I'm around people, I try to hide in the background as much as possible. I don't engage in conversation unless someone speaks to me directly—and then I keep the conversation as short as possible. I withdraw into my own inner world and can't wait to get home!

Some of these signs can also mean I didn't sleep enough or I'm hungry. But when I ask myself what's going on, I usually know what causes me to feel the way I do.

What signs tell you that you need to be on your own again? Pay attention to them from now on if you're not sure.

To know how much alone time you ideally need, you can also do this: think about having a certain amount of alone time per day or week, and notice how this makes you feel. Imagine having thirty minutes of alone time each day, for example. Close your eyes and notice what you feel. Does it feel heavy, constricted, contracted? Thirty minutes per day is not right for you. Does it feel light, open, and you experience a sense of relief? Thirty minutes per day is perfect for you. You can do this exercise in several ways. Check how much solitude you'd like per day. Or check how many days / hours you need to be on your own per week.

When you have some idea of how much alone time you need, you can start changing your schedule. You'll know what to say "yes" to and what to say "no" to.

One thing I know for myself, for example, is that I need space between appointments. Some people feel good about making back-to-back appointments. I don't. I need some time to unwind and process before I'm ready to be present for the next meeting. This is quite common for introverts, so you may need this, too. If so, determine how much time you would like in between meetings. For me, it's a minimum of thirty minutes.

If you have *no* clue how much alone time you need, give yourself some extra time daily or weekly. Try it out. Experiment. How does it feel? How do you enjoy spending that time? Would you like even more time for yourself?

Of course, you can also desire to talk with people more often! Do you sometimes feel that you lack interaction and connection with others? If so, how can you tell? What signs show you that you need to be around people?

We all need a balance between being alone and connecting with others. What that balance looks like is unique for each individual.

Introvert Introspections:

- How can you tell when you're peopled out?
- What helps you recharge when that happens?
- How can you tell when need to be around people?
- How can you make that connection?

Chapter 2

Clarity

Creating a business you love starts with clarity. What does a business you're in love with look like? People often get stuck here. They know what they no longer want, but what they *do* want isn't clear. Think about this question: if anything was possible, you feared nothing, and you trusted that everything always works out for you beautifully, what would you want? (And if that still doesn't give you more insights, ask yourself how you want to feel. As I wrote in Part Two, Chapter 19, *Choose How You Want to Feel*, that's all you need to know.)

When I work with my private clients, I always check the following areas to make sure *every* aspect of their business makes them happy. Take some time to go over each of these areas. Pay attention to the ideas, thoughts, and feelings that come up while you explore each topic. **Forget about what *seems* realistic or impossible.** You don't have to make any changes yet. You're only exploring what you *truly* want. Don't censor yourself and don't judge anything that comes up. It's simply information, and no one has to know your answers.

Clients

Are you working with your ideal clients? Ideal clients are people you love to work with, and they love working with you. Connecting with them makes you happy! Is that how you feel about your current clients? If not, take some time to explore what your ideal client looks like. Describe the person you love to hang out with. That description applies to your ideal clients, too. My own ideal clients are smart, ambitious women with a good sense of humor, for example. They're driven and want to make a difference, but not at their own expense. They take responsibility for their actions and results. They're open-minded, spiritual, and intuitive. They love life and know that they are the creators of their own reality. They're willing to dive deep and face their fears and their dreams. They want to create the business and life of their dreams on their own terms, in their own way.

Write down who *you* love to work with. (Hint: your ideal clients are a lot like you!) Add the issues, problems, or topics you most enjoy working on. What kind of work do you love to do with, or for, your clients? Finally, explore *how* you love to work with your clients. Do you want to work with them online or offline? Do you want to communicate with them via email, voice messages, or videos? Do you prefer working with them one-to-one or in a group setting?

Once you know who your ideal clients are, decide to *only* work with them. This contributes to your happiness and to that of your clients. You deliver your best work when you love what you do and work with people you love!

Plus, why would you want to spend time with people you don't genuinely care about? You're the boss, remember? *You* decide who you work with. No one else has any say in that.

Don't worry about excluding people by choosing to work with only your ideal clients. Yes, you're excluding people from working with you. But A) you ALWAYS do that, anyway. No matter how hard you work, there's a limit to how many people you can work with. And B) you're not friends with everyone with a pulse either, are you? You're picky about who you hang out with, too, right? So why not pick who you prefer to work with as well? **Don't forget: you deliver your BEST work when you're happy.**

The work you do

Do you (still) love what you do? If not, what would you love to do instead? (If you don't know, focus on the feeling you want to get from your work.)

Schedule / lifestyle

Do you love your life? Do you spend your time on activities you love? Do you spend your time with people you love? Do you have enough alone time? Do you have enough time for everything that makes you happy?

Your services / products / offers / whatever it is you sell

Do you like *every* aspect of it? Do you love the content? The price? The way you deliver your product or service?

Your marketing

How do you promote what you do? How does that make you feel? Does your marketing align with your values? With your personality?

Your team / suppliers

Are you happy with your employees, suppliers, or freelancers that work for you? Are you happy with your bookkeeper, assistant, the company who maintains your website, your cleaner? If not, what needs to change? (Don't be afraid to fire someone or stop hiring them. I know this can be hard. But working with someone you're no longer happy with or who doesn't perform well takes a lot of energy. It also costs you money.)

Gather your courage and tell them what you expect. Fire them if they can't deliver what you ask for. Don't make it personal. This is your business, and you pay them. They're not doing you a favor!

Introvert Introspections:

- Think about all these different areas of your business. Notice every single thing that doesn't feel right. What exactly feels off? What would make you feel great about this instead?

Chapter 3

Know Your Non-Negotiables

What do you absolutely *need* to feel happy, whole, and complete? What are you not willing to compromise on? Make sure you know what those things are and then don't compromise on them. This is a crucial part of creating your ideal business and lifestyle. If you don't know what you need to be happy, you'll end up compromising your happiness all the time.

One thing you need to honor are your most important values. If you don't honor them, you'll always feel bad. Your top three values need to be on your list of non-negotiables!

My top three values are freedom, fun, and flow. If one of these elements is missing, I'm not doing it. Or I check what needs to change, and I make those changes.

I automatically check *everything* I do to make sure it matches my values. If something feels even slightly off, I explore what's wrong and if there's something that will make it feel right. If not, I don't do it.

I have other non-negotiables besides my top three values. I work with my ideal clients only, as I mentioned before. Another non-negotiable is the amount of alone time I need.

There are also things I prefer but that I'm willing to make exceptions on. I'd rather not make appointments in the evening, for example. But when I had the chance to be interviewed on a podcast

I loved and this could only happen in the evening due to time zone differences, I happily made an exception.

Here are some examples of non-negotiables from some of my clients. These might inspire you to come up with your own necessary conditions:

- No appointments on Fridays
- Picking the kids up from school at least once a week
- Not working on weekends

Know what you're willing to compromise on, and what you'll *never* settle for. Compromising your non-negotiables eats away at you. You can't go against your values and deepest needs long term. The price is just too high.

Introvert Introspection:

- What do you need to feel happy and fulfilled?

Make a list of all the things that matter to you. Add your most important values. Once your list is complete, decide for each item if this is something you're willing to compromise on. If not, honor these non-negotiables.

Chapter 4

Be Mindful How You Spend Your Time

There's often a discrepancy between what people *say* matters to them and what they *actually* spend their time on. But you can't create a life you love if your priorities and how you spend your time don't match up.

Here's an exercise I regularly give my private coaching clients. First I ask them to make a list of things they deeply care about. What do they value? What makes them genuinely happy? I ask them to choose the five most important things and rank them from 1 (most important) to 5 (least important).

After their list is done, they track how they spend their time for a week. They set a stopwatch and record how much time they spend on *everything* they do: watching TV; answering emails; doing household chores, etc. They record *everything*. I urge them to be honest and to approach this exercise with an open, curious mind—no judgment and no self-criticism. The goal of this exercise is not to find fault or feel bad about yourself. The goal is to bring awareness to what you spend your time—your life!—on. **You can't change what you're not aware of.** Once you know what you *really* spend your time on, you can start making changes so you can spend most of your time on what matters to you most.

This exercise is eye opening. It becomes crystal clear how much time they spend on things that don't truly matter to them. Many people put "family" and "friends" high on their priorities list, for example, but when they see how much time they *actually* spend with them, it's not as much as they'd like. It also becomes very clear how much you prioritize yourself and your dreams (or don't).

Tracking your activities brings other insights, too. People often underestimate how much time certain chores take. They don't realize how much time they spend on social media, for example, or how long they take to do their admin. Making this list shows you where you can save time, how you can spend your time differently, and which tasks or jobs you could delegate to others.

I invite you to do this exercise too. It's insightful to see how you spend your time (your life!)

, and if you spend it on things that truly matter. Once you know how you spend your time, it's easier to see what needs to change to create more freedom, time, and space.

Introvert Introspections:

- Make a list of things that truly matter to you, and include activities you love to spend time on.
- Then, track *everything* you do for a week. Every smartphone has a built-in stopwatch. Record how much time you spend reading, eating, cooking, answering emails, creating invoices, etc. When I say track everything, I mean *everything*!
- At the end of the week, add everything up: how much time do you watch TV per day? And how many hours per week? How much time do you spend answering emails per day? Per week? How much time do you spend playing games with your children, connecting with friends, daydreaming, taking walks, doing admin, cleaning your house, shopping, writing, etc.?

- Finally, take a good look at your timetable. Are you happy with how you spend your time—your life? Do you spend enough time on things and people you love? Do you spend enough time on your priorities? If not, what needs to change? Which changes can you implement right away?

Chapter 5

Your Ideal Schedule—Start Exploring

You can create your schedule any way you like. You truly can! I'm living proof of that. And I've helped my clients create their ideal schedules for years now, too. I know it can be done. I also know it can be tricky. Why? Because ALL your doubts, beliefs, and stories about productivity, making money, or what you feel you're worth, will come up. You need to say "no" and set boundaries—skills that are often underdeveloped. You need to honor your wants, needs, and desires. You need to prioritize *yourself*. That often takes practice as well.

I'll take you through the steps to create your ideal schedule in the next chapters. But first, you need to know what your ideal schedule looks like. To inspire you, I'll share what my typical workdays look like. **Pay attention to your reactions to my schedule.** These are a valuable source of information for the way *you'd* like to structure your days and weeks! Make notes while you read. When something resonates with you, ask yourself: what is it about this that resonates? What is it that speaks to you *exactly*? When you think "I want that, too!," write it down. Pay attention to what you dislike as well. What *exactly* don't you like? What would you prefer instead?

My typical week

Here's what a typical workweek and workday look like for me. I wake up when I'm rested, without an alarm clock. The only time I set an alarm is when I have an appointment at 10 a.m. to make sure I have time to myself before I speak with someone. I'm usually awake before the alarm goes off, but it brings me peace of mind to know I won't oversleep.

The first things I do when I'm awake is journal and drink tea in bed. I get out of bed when I feel like getting up. Sometimes this is directly after I finished journaling. Sometimes I get my laptop and start working in bed: answering client emails, writing blog posts, posting on social media, working on a book. Around 11 a.m. I work out—from home, of course, so I don't have to go to a gym and be around people. ;-) After that I break my fast. In the afternoon, I go for a walk.

Other than that, I have no agenda. I do whatever feels inspired in each moment. I don't make plans. I don't think of my time in terms of "work days" or "off days." I simply do whatever feels right the moment it feels inspired, regardless of what day or time it is. I'm writing this chapter at 9 p.m. on a Saturday, for example. Some people wouldn't do that, because they don't work weekends. If that's you, by all means, honor that. For me, it doesn't matter what day or time it is. If I feel inspired to write on Saturday night, I write. If I feel inspired to do absolutely nothing on Monday afternoon, I do absolutely nothing on Monday afternoon.

I make a maximum of four appointments per week. These include ALL work-related meetings: podcast interviews, sales conversations, client calls, live group calls, calls with my coach, etc. I plan these appointments on Tuesday, Wednesday or Thursday between 10 a.m. at the earliest and 6 p.m. at the latest. I plan two appointments per day at most. Every fourth week is my hermit week. This is my completely appointment-free week.

When I have appointments, my days look pretty much the same. I journal, workout, take a walk, write, answer emails, follow my flow in each moment. Somewhere in between, I have those appointments. All of which are online. I see no one face-to-face besides family and friends. (Most of my closest friends don't live in The Netherlands. But I even rarely meet my Dutch friends in person. I usually talk to them on the phone.)

Besides those four work-related appointments, I make some personal appointments. Never more than one per weekend, and not every weekend.

I always take two weeks off in December / January and three or four weeks in August / September.

This is what my ideal schedule, my ideal LIFE, looks like at the moment. (It might change.) What does yours look like?

Start exploring

Give yourself time to explore what you want. Often, the first things you come up with aren't your *genuine* desires. Your first ideas are usually the things you *think you can get.* If you give yourself time to ponder, what you *truly* want can surface.

When I thought about how many appointments I wanted to make per week, for example, the first number I came up with was eight. However, the number I eventually landed on was four.

This question can help you determine what you genuinely love: if *anything* is possible, if you feared nothing, and if you trusted that you will always have enough money, what would feel ideal for you? How do you love to spend your time? How do you love to live?

Creating your ideal schedule is all about creating your ideal *life.* It's about how you choose to spend your time on earth and who you want to spend it with. What do you want to do in the time that you have? Who do you want to be with? And how do you choose to *feel?*

Introvert Introspections:

- As you read through my descriptions, what did you notice?
- What spoke to you? What did you like or dislike? What does that tell you about what you'd like YOUR days and weeks to look like?
- What does your ideal schedule look like?

Don't censor what comes up. Dismiss nothing because it feels unrealistic or undoable. You have NO idea what's possible when you set your mind to it! Besides, it's a step-by-step process. Something that's not doable today may be easy next year!

On www.bookfreebees.com, you can sign up for bonus gifts, including an Ideal Schedule Worksheet. This worksheet helps you explore what your ideal schedule looks like.

Chapter 6

Your Ideal Schedule— Doubts and Dreams

When you explore what your ideal lifestyle looks like, doubts and fears can come up. Is this really possible? Can you make enough money and grow your business this way?

Doubts also often come up when you make changes to your schedule and business. **It's normal for doubts to show up.** Everyone has them! Your doubts are NOT a sign to give up or water down your desires. Doubts simply show you that you have thoughts and beliefs that contradict your desires. Your job is not to forget about your desires. Your job is to face your doubts so they no longer have power over you. When you *suppress* your doubts, they unconsciously determine your actions and block your path forward. When you're *not aware* of your doubts, they'll block your path forward as well! That's why it's important to face your doubts and bring them out into the open. I described my own doubts in Part One, *Chapter 10, The Hardest Changes to Make.* Here are some more examples of doubts my clients encountered. Read through them and see if anything resonates.

One of my clients wanted to spend Wednesday afternoons with her kids. She worried taking time off would hurt her business. Another client wanted to work *longer* hours instead of fewer. She felt guilty for that desire. Did this make her a terrible mother? Other examples of doubts my clients experienced:

- Will my clients accept this?
- What will my partner / family / friends / peers / clients think of this?
- Can I make enough money / grow my business when I do this?
- I can't possibly delegate this.
- It's impossible to cut back on those activities / hours.
- No one else does it this way. That must mean it's impossible.

Perhaps none of these doubts sound familiar to you. Maybe you have no doubts at all! That's certainly possible. Just be aware that doubts, fears, or questions *might* come up.

Sometimes your doubts come up so quickly that you have no space left to explore what you want. To prevent that, give yourself permission to dream. Give yourself permission to want what you want and to receive it, too! Tell yourself that *all* you do right now is dream. You're not deciding or changing anything yet. And you don't have to implement anything you come up with. You can relax, you're only dreaming! This soothes your fears and opens a space that allows you to feel, imagine, wish, hope, and dream.

Introvert Introspections:

- What, if any, doubts come up for you when you think about your ideal schedule? Write them down.
- Go over each doubt. Are you 100 percent certain this will happen? Can you come up with at least *one* reason this doubt might not be true?

Chapter 7
Your Ideal Schedule—Implementing

Once you know what your ideal schedule looks like, you can implement it. You don't need crystal clarity on how you want to spend every moment of every day. If all you know is that you want to take two hours off each Friday, then that's what you start with. If all you know is how you want to feel, that's enough, too. All you need to know now is exactly what you know now! New desires (and actions) will show up when you're ready for them.

Creating your ideal schedule starts with these two steps. (Hint: creating ANYTHING starts with these two steps.)

1. Know what you want, and
2. decide that this is how it will be.

That's exactly what I did. I *decided* I would make my ideal schedule work. Did I still have doubts? Yes! Was I worried it wouldn't be possible or I wouldn't be able to make enough money? Yes! Did I still feel weird and slightly ashamed about the way I wanted to live and do business? Yes! Did I know *how* I was going to make it all work? No!

But I knew I was no longer willing to tolerate a less than ideal business, schedule, or life.

I reminded myself that I have NO idea what's possible. Neither do you! **What your limited mind can imagine is *nothing* compared to what your soul can come up with.**

Take a stand for what you want. Decide to have it. Let your soul and the universe figure out the details. Keep faith, keep imagining that what you want is already yours, and keep following your intuition and inner nudges. That's how I created a business and life filled with extreme freedom and space. You will create your ideal business, too, if you take a stand for what you want and stop tolerating anything less!

The practical steps WILL show up for you one by one. You will recognize them because deep down you *feel* and *know* what to do. It may take time. Especially if a lot needs to change. But it *will* happen if you don't give up and keep taking steps!

Some of the steps you feel called to take are directly linked to creating your ideal schedule, for example, to block off each Friday in your calendar to prevent you from making appointments that day. Other steps may not seem related to creating your ideal schedule at all, for example, when you feel inspired to sign up for a photography course. Do it anyway. This step may have nothing to do with changing your schedule, but you can be certain it's related to creating a life you love! Your soul knows how to bring you everything you want and need exactly when you need it. Choose to trust that and follow your inner nudges and intuition *always*.

As far as practical steps go, these are some steps that helped me implement my ideal schedule. How *you* make *your* ideal business work may look very different, so don't think you have to do anything I did. Let your intuition guide you on your path. The steps *you* have to take *will* show up for you, I guarantee it!

Raising fees

I raised my fees for private coaching. This meant that even though I worked with fewer private clients, my income from private coaching stayed the same.

Group programs

I added group programs. Working with groups is a great way to leverage your time. You can reach more people in the same time (or even less).

Products

After I deliver an online program live once, I sell the recordings as a finished product. People can purchase them and go through the content without it costing me *any* time. It's all automated.

Books

Books are a great way to share your message and make money without having to interact with people. But that's not the reason I write books. I write books because I was born to write!

Stick to the new schedule

I made *no* exceptions to my new four-appointments-per-week maximum, especially at the beginning. If there were already four appointments on my calendar, I didn't make a fifth. Making exceptions is a slippery slope. If you continue to make them, you'll never get what you want. So I was super strict about it!

Another thing I did was to become even pickier about the appointments I made. I ONLY plan an appointment when it feels 100 percent right.

Next steps

These are the steps you need to take to create your ideal schedule.

1. Dream. What is it you REALLY want? What makes your heart sing?
2. Decide. Decide to get what you want. Commit to doing whatever it takes for as long as it takes.
3. Brainstorm. What are one to three steps you can come up with that will make your current schedule a bit more ideal for you? Implement those. After that, the next step will come up. It will! Take one step and the rest of your path unfolds after that, step by step.

If fears and doubts come up, see if a chapter in this book can help you out. If you have a hard time setting boundaries, saying "no," or prioritizing yourself and your needs, check out my book *The Art of Divine Selfishness - transform your life, your business & the world by putting YOU first.* (You can read all about it at www.divinelyselfish. com.)

Remember, there's *always* a way to do *everything* your way. Once you're clear on the *inside* and take a stand for what you want, the *outer* steps will fall into place.

Introvert Introspections:

*   What are one to three steps you can take that will make your schedule more ideal for you?
*   When will you take them?

Chapter 8

Hermit-Friendly Marketing

It's never been easier to market your business in introvert-friendly ways than now. When I started my business, this wasn't the case. Social media was pretty much nonexistent in 2003. The main way to let people know about my work was visiting networking events. I HATED that with a vengeance! There were other ways to market a business, like advertising, but the most common (and free!) ways to market a business involved interacting with people.

These days, it's easy to let people know about your work without ever leaving your house or talking to anyone. Thank god for the internet; what a blessing for introverts! You can promote your business on social media, via podcasts, blogs, delivering (free) online webinars or seminars, writing articles and sending them to people who subscribed to your email list … and you can do all this from your home, in your pajamas, if you like. The opportunities to market your business in ways that are introvert friendly and a good match to your personality are endless!

So, how do you determine what works best for you? Start by looking at what you love to do and are good at (or you're willing to learn more about), and use that as the basis for your marketing. I love writing and speaking, so these are the basis of my marketing. I write newsletters and blog posts. I host my own podcast and am a guest on other people's podcasts. I also deliver free online masterclasses and make the occasional video. I'm active on social media and like to connect with people there. That way, I can connect in my own time, from my home, and I can spend as much or as little time connecting as I like.

Whatever you like to do, there's *always* a way to incorporate it in your marketing. You can interact with people as much or as little as you like. If your work requires a lot of sales conversations, you can hire others to do that for you. You can even hire people to do your marketing for you if you *really* dislike it. Or you can shift your perspective on marketing.

I absolutely *hated* marketing when I had just started my business. Not only because it felt salesy and inauthentic but also because I was scared to death to make myself visible. That was a BIG fear that stopped me from promoting my work. Slowly but surely, I overcame that fear. Shifting my perspective on marketing helped me with that, and I even learned to enjoy marketing!

Now, I don't really think about marketing as something I do to promote my business anymore. I see marketing as a way to express myself. Looking at it that way is incredibly motivating for me. Another shift in my perspective was to look at marketing as a way to be of value. I use my marketing to share my message and inspire people. That way I can make a difference even if people never buy anything from me! It also helped to realize that *no one* could benefit from my work if they didn't know about me or how I could help them.

The most important thing to remember about marketing is this: be true to yourself, show the real you, play to your strengths, and focus on what you love and enjoy. When you do that, you'll be fine.

Last but not least: don't overcomplicate it. Marketing is simply letting people know what you offer.

Introvert Introspections:

- What do you like to do? Writing / speaking / making videos / drawing / painting / talking with people / inspiring others / sharing resources and wisdom …
- What are you excited about and want to share in the content of your work and / or your message? What's something you wish everyone knew? What can you talk about for hours?
- What motivates you to share your work with others? Why do you do what you do? What difference do you love to make? How could your marketing help you fulfill your mission?

Chapter 9

General Tips to Free Up
Time and Interact Less

Here are some more tips to free up time in your business and in your schedule. I mentioned some of them before but include them here to give you a complete overview.

Create products

You can create physical products like books, card decks, journals, candles, jewelry, or whatever fits your business. You can also turn your courses into online products.

Group programs

This is a great way to leverage your time. Instead of reaching one person per hour, you can now reach a thousand people per hour, or twenty, or any number you like. You can add group Q&A calls and / or an online forum where people can ask questions. You can deliver your group programs on- or offline. I deliver *all* my work online because that's what I love most. You can deliver your work in any way *you* prefer.

Hire someone to deliver coaching / support to your clients

You don't have to do everything yourself! Even when you think you're the only one who can do what you do. ;-) You can hire someone to support people in your group programs. You can hire co-trainers or co-coaches. You can train others to work with your clients so you can reach more people without working more.

Hire someone to do your sales conversations

This can save you a lot of time!

Delegate and outsource

Delegating tasks you don't like or aren't good at is a big time saver. You can outsource absolutely everything, from doing your admin to answering phones and emails, and from doing sales conversations to coaching. (And don't forget everything you can outsource in your personal life!)

I choose to delegate everything I don't like and / or I'm not good at. I have a great virtual assistant who answers my emails, maintains my website, makes sales pages, etc. I have a bookkeeper who does my admin. This saves me a lot of time and energy.

If it feels scary to hire an assistant, start small and work your way up from there. That's how I did it, too.

Automate and streamline

This can save you so much time! There are many apps and software programs that can help you with this. My shopping cart automatically creates invoices and gives people access to their content, for example. I don't have to do any of that manually. The possibilities to automate recurring tasks are endless!

Work online instead of face-to-face

This is a huge time saver! You don't have to travel, make coffee, or clean up your office. You don't have to engage in small talk before or after your meeting. Heaven!

Be mindful of how you spend your time

Prioritize yourself, your self-care, and everything else that truly matters to you. Be mindful of how you spend your time and who you spend it with. Cut out everything that doesn't bring you joy, love, pleasure, or contributes to your goals and dreams.

Batch tasks

One of my former coaches advised me to batch my work. What she meant by that was to do specific tasks on specific days. For example: write all your copy (blogs, emails, etc.) on Friday mornings between 10 a.m. and noon. Do your admin on Thursdays between 4 p.m. and 4:30 p.m.

I never did this. I'm sure it saves time, but I don't like to plan what I do when. I prefer to do things when they feel inspired, not when my schedule tells me it's time for it. You can try this, though; it's a solid strategy to work more efficiently!

There are more things you can do to free up time, but I'm no expert at time management. It's a topic I'm not interested in, and I deliberately created a way to live and do business that doesn't require me to learn about it either. If you're looking for smart, practical ways to free up time, just search the internet for time management tips.

> *Introvert Introspection:*
>
> - What can you do, change, or let go of to free up time? Make a list of *every* option you can think of, whether or not it seems doable. See if you can come up with ten different things. For example, spend less time on social media, check your email less frequently, order your groceries online, hire an assistant for specific tasks, etc.

Pick one to three things you will implement this week. (Then implement the rest of the items on your list one or two at a time every week after that.)

PART FOUR

Troubleshooting

Introduction

As I've mentioned several times, the *practical* aspect of creating a thriving business and life you love is the simple part. The hard part is the inner work: the doubts and fears that come up when you make changes and pursue a new dream. Letting doubts and fears stop you is the number one reason people settle for what they have and never go for their *true* dreams. They're not willing to tackle their inner obstacles or think (mistakenly!) they can't overcome them. This is not true. You're more powerful than you think!

Over the years, I've seen the same fears come up for my clients the moment they dreamed about their ideal business (or the moment they implemented that dream). I experienced most of these fears myself, too!

Chances are you'll recognize one or more of them, too. If nothing bothers you, skip this part of the book! Just remember to come back if uncertainties arise or you feel scared to move forward. One of these chapters can probably help you through.

Chapter 1

Fear of Criticism

Criticism is something many people fear. When I ask my clients what *exactly* they fear, they usually have to think about it. Because, really, what makes this fear such a big deal?

The main reason negative feedback hurts is that it triggers something in you that doesn't feel good. It can trigger the fear that you're not good enough or that you're doing something wrong. Disapproval can activate a negative feeling you already have about yourself. It can feed your doubts about yourself or your work.

It's usually not the critique itself that hurts you. *It's what you already fear, doubt, or feel uncertain about that gets activated inside you.*

The solution is *not* to avoid everything that might trigger negative comments. **The solution is to heal what you feel bad about within yourself.** What is it you doubt, fear, or don't feel good about? Face it. Then, heal it by loving the part of yourself that's fearful and uncertain.

I used to be afraid to openly talk or write about spiritual topics, for example. I would only mention the words "intuition" or "soul" when I worked with someone privately and was certain they would understand what I was talking about. I didn't use these words for a long time on my website or in my blog articles for fear of being criticized or losing (potential) clients. Until I realized that it had become impossible for me to work with people who weren't open to spirituality. I knew I had to start writing and talking about my own spiritual side, but before I could do that, I had to come to terms with my spirituality first. It wasn't that I feared that *others* would think I was crazy—I just hadn't fully accepted this part of myself yet.

Criticism can still sting even after you've healed your self-criticisms and feelings about yourself! But it will no longer stop you from being true to yourself and your dreams.

What also helps is to realize that other's opinions say more about them than about you. Their opinion is a projection of *their* mindset, wounds, preferences, feelings, dreams, fears, etc. (The same goes for compliments, by the way! These aren't personal either, and say more about others than about you, too.) Take nothing personal. At its core, it never is.

Again, critique can still hurt. When it does, give yourself space to feel your emotions and let them out. Don't suppress your feelings. That's never a good idea. Just don't let your fear of criticism stop you. Yes, it can hurt. But you can deal with that. Adjusting or shrinking yourself or your dreams hurts you much more in the end.

Introvert Introspections:

- If the fear of negative feedback no longer stopped you from following your dreams, what, if anything, would be different?
- What would you do?
- What would you stop doing?

Chapter 2

Fear That You Can't Be Like That

This is the fear that you're not good enough. The fear that you fall short or should be different than you are. The fear that you're too much or not enough.

These fears and doubts can come up when you decide to shape your business around who you truly are. I noticed it myself and see it in my clients as well. As soon as they even *think* about creating their business *exactly* as they want to, they wonder, is it really okay to want this? Is it really okay to be like this? Am I really okay? My answers are always the same: yes. Yes. And yes.

You are who you are for a reason. Who you are born to be is exactly who you need to be to fulfill your purpose and contribute to others. **You are who you are because that's who you're supposed to be.** Every human being has something unique to contribute, and the way to make a difference is to just be yourself.

Introvert Introspections:

- What, if anything, would change for you if you believed that you are *exactly* as you're meant to be, and *nothing* about you was wrong or flawed?
- What if the thing you think is wrong or weird about you is actually one of your greatest strengths, talents, or qualities? What, if anything, would change for you?

    For example: I see my introversion as one of my top three qualities and strengths now. Because I'm rested and happy, I can give the best of myself to others. Because I take a lot of time to ponder and reflect, I gather wisdom and inspiration I can share with others via my books and online programs. Because I am unapologetically who I am and live the way I choose to live, I inspire others to do the same.

- How could what makes you different or weird be *your* greatest asset?

Chapter 3

Fear That You Can Have
Either This OR That

This is the fear that having what you want comes at a price. The fear that you can't have *everything* you want.

I used to fear I had to choose between freedom OR success. I didn't believe I could have both. That's why I had enough money *or* enough alone time but never enjoyed both simultaneously. **I had one or the other because it never occurred to me I could have both.**

Once I realized *I believed* I had to choose between freedom *or* success, I chose *both*. I decided I could have *everything* I wanted. Why would that be impossible?

My clients often think they have to choose between several things that are important to them, too. Society and their upbringing taught them they could have one *or* the other. As long as they (unconsciously) believe that they have to choose between two or more desires, they aren't able to receive *everything* they want. They feel stuck and unable to realize *all* their dreams because they don't believe they can make them all real.

Here are some common things people often think they have to choose between. You may recognize one or more of them.

- Being ethical OR rich.

- Being a good mother OR a successful entrepreneur.
- Being successful OR having a loving relationship.
- Growing your business OR having enough time for yourself.
- Being rich OR doing purposeful work and making a positive difference.
- Being true to yourself OR growing your business.

You don't have to choose between any of these. You can have it all! **The ONLY reason you can't have everything you want is your belief that you can't.**

You can solve this issue by changing your mind. One way I did this was to *decide* to have everything I wanted. Another thing I did was to turn my doubts into positive affirmations. Every morning, I wrote these affirmations in my journal. While I wrote them, I focused on how each affirmation made me *feel*. How would I act that day if I believed this affirmation? What decisions would I make? What would my perspective be?

I repeated this process daily until my new affirmation felt natural and normal and there was no need to repeat it any more.

Here's how I came up with my affirmations. First, I wrote down my doubt. Then I turned it into a positive statement that described what I wanted to believe instead. For example, one of my doubts was: I will lose my freedom when I reach more people. I turned this into the following affirmation, "The more people I reach, the freer I am."

Try it. Write down one of your doubts and turn it into a positive statement. It's okay if you don't believe it yet, **as long as you're excited or curious if it *could* be true.** Without excitement, curiosity, or willingness to find out if your new belief could become real, your affirmation won't work. If your statement triggers negative thoughts, cynicism, or more doubts, it will only make you feel worse. Play with your affirmations until they invoke a positive feeling.

Another thing you can do is come up with three to five reasons your new belief or affirmation could be *as true* or even *truer* than your doubt. Here's the list of reasons I came up with to prove that *The more people I reach, the freer I am* could be as true or truer than *The more people I reach, the less free I feel.*

- When I reach more people, I make more money and I can delegate answering my emails to my assistant.
- I can delegate and outsource more in general, which frees up more time.
- One of my coaches told me she feels freer since her business is bigger. (If she experiences this, I can experience it, too!)
- Reaching more people leads to more income, which leads to less stress, which makes me feel freer.

Introvert Introspections:

- Do you believe you have to give up something to create your ideal business and lifestyle? What, if anything, do you think the cost will be?
- Could it be possible that you DON'T have to give that up or pay that price? What if you could have BOTH? Can you come up with three to five reasons that could be true? (You don't need scientific proof! Your fears and doubts aren't backed by scientific evidence, either.)

Chapter 4

Fear That You Can't Get What You Want

As we grow up, most of us *unlearn* to follow our desires. Even when you don't feel like it, you have to go to school. You have to learn math if you want to or not. You have to go to bed when you're not tired, sit down when you want to run around, and eat vegetables you dislike.

This teaches you that it's not always possible to get everything you want. That your desires are unimportant or impossible to fulfill. Another message this can give you is that your needs don't matter—other people's needs come first.

As a result, you can lose touch with your dreams and needs. What's the point of wanting something if you can't get it?

But you're in a different position now. You're no longer a child who has to obey the rules your parents or teachers set for you. You're an adult. YOU are in charge of your happiness, your dreams, your business, and your life. You're the boss! You decide *everything* now, and you can make your own rules. You want Mondays off? You take Mondays off. You want to pick up your children from school each day? Go for it! You don't want that? Don't do it!

You're in charge. It's *your* business and *your* life. YOU decide! Give yourself permission to want what you want, and to get it, too. You started your business to be free, so use that freedom. It's your business and your life, so make it as good as you can.

You can achieve *anything* you set your mind to, even when it seems impossible now.

Can you give yourself permission to want what you want and to receive it as well—even when you're not sure if it's possible or how you can achieve it?

> *Introvert Introspection:*
>
> - Can you think of three to five reasons it *is* possible to get what you want?

Chapter 5

Fear That You Can't Grow Your Business Your Way

I mentioned before that I stopped setting goals and making business plans several years ago. When I told people about that, many of them said that wasn't possible. You can't grow your business without goals and plans, can you?

I used to believe that, too. But I learned that this is not true. You *can* grow your business without setting goals or making plans. I do it that way, so apparently it's possible! I now believe that there's only *one* thing you need to grow your business and get anything else you want and need, and that is to follow your intuition. That's really all you need to do! Of course, your intuition can guide you to set goals or make plans, if that's something that's a good fit for you. For me, however, it isn't.

I'll repeat what I mentioned before:

There are as many ways to grow your business as there are entrepreneurs. **What works for you is determined by what you *believe* will work for you, *not* by what others think is necessary.** Dare to follow what feels right for *you*, and don't get distracted by other's opinions. You can grow your business in numerous ways. Your intuition will point you to the way that works for you. Stop listening to others and start listening to your own inner wisdom instead. Your intuition *never* steers you wrong. You can always trust that.

Introvert Introspections:

- If you trusted your intuition and inner guidance on what's right for you, what would you do?
- What would you stop doing?
- What advice or "rules" would you ignore from now on if you trusted your inner knowing?

Chapter 6

Fear That You Can't Make Enough Money

There are many ways to make money. You can make money doing the craziest things! As long as there are people who see the value of what you do and will pay for it, you can make money with it.

I once read an article about someone who had a thriving business in … standing in line for others! This guy walked outside one day and saw people lined up to get movie tickets. He noticed people stood in line for hours and thought: what if you could hire someone to stand in line for you? He figured there were plenty of people who would be willing to pay for that service. Long story short: he ended up with a successful business (with several employees!) in standing in line.

People make money in the weirdest ways. You'll never know if you can make money doing something if you don't try! If you receive an idea, chances are there are people who are interested in it.

There are limitless ways the universe can bring money to you. Your business is a *channel* through which money can come to you, but it's not the *source* of money. There's only *one* source of money: the universe.

Do what you feel called to do, be true to who you are, follow your joy, and the money will follow. It can come through your business, your partner, winning the lottery, investments, and endless other ways that you can't even come up with.

Choose to trust that life always takes care of you. It does! Life has always carried you and will continue to do so.

Introvert Introspections:

- If you trusted you will always have enough money, what would you do?
- What would you stop doing?
- If you trusted that life always carries you, how would that feel? What would change?

Chapter 7

Fear That You Don't Know What Your Way of Doing Business Is

You know you want to do business in your own way. But you're not always sure what that looks like. You may know that you don't want to go to networking events, for example. Or that you don't want to work online. But you're not sure what you want instead. Now what?

First, it's good to know what you *don't* want. Knowing what you don't want helps you figure out what it is you *do* want. You may not have clarity yet, but that will come in time!

Second, you don't *have* to know what you want. All you have to do is what feels right in each moment. When you follow your intuition, you automatically walk your own path that brings you everything you want and need. You don't have to know *how* to achieve anything. Your soul knows and will guide you every step of the way. Listen to your intuition. Do what you *know* deep down is right for you. Life will bring you what you need the moment you need it.

When I stopped making business plans and setting goals, as I described in a previous chapter, I had *no idea* what I'd do instead. No clue! I'll just wing it, I thought. Well, it turned out that "just winging it" is my official business strategy now. Most business coaches will tell you this doesn't work. "You can't just wing it!" Why not? It's how I do it. When something feels inspired, I do it—even when it scares me and I don't feel like it. I grow my business in my own way. I feel fantastic about my business, my life, and how I spend my time!

Your way of doing business might look completely different. It doesn't matter. When you follow what feels right for *you*, you automatically do business in *your* own way. You don't have to know in advance what it looks like. It doesn't have to look like anyone else's way and it's okay if it does. Just follow what you know deep down. Don't be afraid to experiment and test things out. That's the best way to find out what works for you.

Introvert Introspections:

- If you trusted everything will always work out for you, how would you ideally want to run and grow your business?
- If you trusted everything will always work out for you, what would you change in your business? What would you do? What would you stop doing?

Chapter 8

Fear That You'll Fail

What if you have a dream but can't make it real? What if you fail? The truth is that you have NO idea what's possible until you try. The only guarantee you have is this: if you stay where you are, you'll *never* know what could have been if you gave your dreams a go.

SO much more is possible than you think! There's always a way to live a fulfilling life and create a business that serves you.

Maybe something doesn't work out. So what? Try something else. Move on. That's part of being an entrepreneur (and part of life!) anyway. Some things work out, some things don't. Other things work out *way* better than you could have ever imagined.

Do you want to look back at a life fully lived? A life where you pursued your dreams and honored everything that truly matters to you? Or would you rather look back at a life where you always played it safe? And you'll never know what could have been if you gave your dreams a shot?

I'd rather take a risk and fail than never even try. That feels like a wasted life to me. Because of that attitude, I've learned that I'm capable of more than I knew. And so much more is possible still!

Please know that taking risks is *not* always necessary to realize your dreams, though! Yes, you may need to do something scary at times, but you can often break down scary actions into small and doable steps.

Keep taking step after step toward your dreams. You'll be surprised at what's possible and how good your life can get. You have nothing to lose and a world to win!

Introvert Introspections:

- What kind of life do you want to look back on? A life fully lived? A life where you took the risk of following your dreams? Or a life where you always played it safe and you'll never know what could have happened if only you tried?
- What if things DO work out? What if you succeed?

Chapter 9

Fear That You'll Be Worse Off

What if you make changes and find that you were happier before? That's easy: you change course and make new choices.

You can never know in advance what you will get and how it will feel. But it *always* pays off to honor your desires. It makes you feel fully alive. It opens you up. Following your dreams brings fresh energy and excitement. It leads to a surge of ideas and inspiration. You learn. You grow. You expand. Following your desires feels fulfilling and opens you up to experiences you haven't had before.

Yes, it's possible that what you end up with is not as satisfying as you think. That's no problem. You simply choose something different.

You never know what becomes possible when you choose to change and take a risk. Let the universe surprise and delight you, and go for it!

Introvert Introspection:

- What would change if you trusted you can always make new choices and nothing is ever lost?

Chapter 10

Fear That You Can't Trust Yourself

Do you doubt if you can *fully* trust yourself, what you do, and how you do it? If so, why? Over the course of your life you already proved multiple times that you are trustworthy, that your instincts are spot on, and that you know what you're doing.

Maybe you didn't always *listen* to your intuition, but you've always had a gut feeling telling you what to do and who to trust. Focus on those moments. Make a list of them if you like. Remember the times your intuition was right. Remember when you just *knew* what you had to do, and it worked out great.

Also write down the times when you *knew* the right thing to do, but you didn't do it. Can you see why you ignored your intuition?

Looking at these examples will teach you two things: that you can trust yourself, and when (and why) you sometimes ignore your intuition. Knowing when you do or don't listen will help you act on your intuition more frequently.

CHOOSE to trust yourself. The more you honor who you are and the way you are, the better you will feel (and the easier your life becomes). The more you become who you *truly* are and let go of everything you're not, the smoother your life becomes. Work with your rhythm instead of against it. Honor the way you naturally do things. Follow your intuition, your joy, and your heart. You can trust it all and you can trust yourself!

If you keep doubting yourself, this exercise can help. Every night, write down three to five things that prove you can trust yourself. Even the littlest things count! Did you pay a bill on time? You can trust yourself to handle your money wisely. You can trust yourself to pay the bills. Did you eat healthy? You can trust yourself to take good care of yourself. Did a client compliment you? You can trust that you did something right.

Introvert Introspections:

- What would it be like to fully trust yourself?
- What would change?
- Can you come up with ten reasons you can trust yourself?

Chapter 11

Fear of Losing People

When I first decided to turn myself from a crappy hermit to a happy hermit, I wasn't sure how my (potential) clients would react. Would my changes make them doubt if they wanted to hire me? Would I lose my clients and never find new ones?

I wasn't sure and felt wobbly about it. But I took the risk anyway. I decided to trust even deeper what I already knew to be true: your true friends *and* your ideal clients love you for who you are, exactly as you are. Your ideal clients are attracted to you *because* you are completely true to yourself.

Even though I knew this to be true, part of me was still worried. So I *chose* to trust that I'd always have clients and my decision wouldn't hurt my business. After all, what was the alternative? To remain a crappy hermit for the rest of my life? To continue feeling like something was missing? No. That was no longer an option. I wasn't available for that anymore. I decided to trust that even if I lost all my clients, new ones would come in. They did!

People who *truly* love you will stay. The ones who fall away no longer resonate with you. Your relationship has gone as far as it could and has fulfilled its purpose. Or they only loved you conditionally. They loved you as long as you were who they wanted you to be. They loved you as long as you gave them what *they* wanted. You don't want these people in your life. It's a good thing if they fall away. They're not good for you and they don't *truly* care about you.

The moment you become who you're born to be and start living the life you were born to live, the people who no longer resonate with you fall away. This falling away might feel sad and you might feel lonely for a while. But it also opens up space for your *true* soulmates to come in: the people who love you for who you are, exactly as you are. They don't want you to be different than you are. They don't need you to betray yourself to please them. Your ideal clients and true friends are people who love you *because* you are who you are. *Because* you do life and business in your way, on your terms. They love you *because* you are YOU.

Introvert Introspections:

- If you were willing to take the risk of losing people or leaving them behind, what would change?
- What would you do? What would you stop doing? What would you let go of?

Chapter 12

Fear That an Ideal Business Isn't Possible for You

You may have read my story and thought: well, Brigitte, I'm glad it worked out for you, but it's impossible for me to create the kind of business you have! It's easy for you to make these changes because you:

- Have no kids
- Have enough money to pay for a virtual team
- Have work that you can leverage
- Are a writer
- Are healthy
- Know how to create online programs
- Work as a coach

I'm sure there are more reasons you could come up with that, in your mind, explain why *I* can do this and *you* can't. Yes, I know that I'm privileged. Yes, I know that some people have it easier than others. And it's definitely easier to create more space for yourself when you don't have kids! (My partner is a co-parent of two children, so I've seen up close how much time and energy raising kids takes.)

Still, I invite you to let go of thinking others have it easier than you. **Focusing on why others have it easier than you *completely* disempowers you.** You're enforcing the belief that something isn't possible for you. You tell yourself you can't do or have something and close the door to opportunities. When you don't believe you have options, you can't see any—even when an opportunity is right under your nose.

Your mind *always* (unconsciously) finds reasons to prove that what you believe is true. If you believe something is impossible, you'll only see proof that something isn't possible. If you believe something is possible, you'll see options and opportunities. (If you don't believe something is possible yet, you can at least become curious to see if it *might* be possible. This opens the door to see solutions to bring you what you want.)

You can't see possibilities when you focus on justifying why you can't have something. You can't see opportunities in your own life when you focus on someone else's life.

Stop looking at others. Instead, explore why you're so keen to explain or defend why you won't be able to create your ideal business or life. The reason for that is usually fear. Fear that you can't have what you want. Fear that you're not capable or worthy of getting what you want. Fear that you will lose something once you have it, so why bother trying to get it?

If you think you can't create a business and life you love, ask yourself this: are you willing to open your mind and become curious about what might be possible for you? If the answer is "yes," there's no need to ask yourself the second question. But if your answer is "no," ask yourself why that is. What, if anything, do you fear or what are you resisting? Why is it important to hold on to the belief that you can't have something? What's the benefit of believing that?

Maybe there are circumstances in your life that make it difficult to make your business 100 percent ideal for you now. But you can at least *explore* what (minor) changes you *can* make. There is always room for improvement, if only a little!

All my clients have different circumstances. Most of my clients have children and a lot less time for themselves than I do. Some are single parents. Some have to take care of a sick relative. Some are sick themselves. They each have their own fears, doubts, and issues to deal with. Their situations are different, but they have ONE thing in common: **they're willing to explore what's possible for them**. They're willing to think and act differently, even when it scares them or it feels highly uncomfortable. Because of that attitude, they can transform more than they *ever* thought possible. They find more freedom in their business and life (and within themselves!) than they *ever* thought they could achieve.

Everyone has their own issues and fears, including me. Yes, I may have it easier than you. But that doesn't mean I didn't have my own shit to deal with. Since I started my business I've been scared shitless, stressed out, and anxious many times. I doubted myself and what I was doing more often than I can remember. But I never gave up. I was determined. I was committed to myself, my life, and my happiness. Above all, I was curious. Curious to see what could be possible if I didn't let my fears and doubts stop me. Aren't you curious to see what's possible for you?

Your dreams may be different from mine. Your fears and issues may be different from mine. My circumstances may be easier than yours. But you can dream. You can explore what you desire. You can decide to go for your dreams, no matter what. You can open your mind and become curious to see what's possible for you. You can ask for help from others, from your soul, and from the universe. You can hire a coach. Or come up with another way to get help if you can't afford a coach. Or come up with ways to get money to pay for a coach.

You can learn to move through your fears and build your confidence. You can learn the practical knowledge and skills you may need. You can take action and make decisions and you can do SO MUCH MORE THAN YOU THINK if only you give yourself a chance to find out.

That's what I did. And that's what *you* can do, too. Remember: there's *always* a way to do business *your* way. There's *always* a way to make your business and life better and more beautiful, no matter how bad or good it currently is.

Are you willing to see what's possible for you? Are you willing to surprise yourself? Are you willing to prioritize yourself, your dream, your LIFE? If so, the sky is not even the limit, baby. The only limits are the limits of your thoughts. And you can *always* shift those!

Introvert Introspections:

- What would you change, do, or stop doing if you believed everything is possible and everything will always work out perfectly for you?
- What would change if you were at least willing to become curious about what might be possible for you?

Chapter 13

The Root Fear That Stops You from Doing Business and Life 100 percent YOUR Way

The root of the fears that can come up about doing business and life in your way, on your terms, is this: that it's impossible to be *completely* true to yourself and do business and life *exactly* as you want to, and still thrive. (Or even survive! You'd be surprised how many people feel that being themselves in this world is unsafe and leaves them poor and alone. I used to fear that myself.)

Growing up, most of us received messages that we can't be completely ourselves in this world—let alone in a work environment. We learned that to make money, we need to be and behave differently. We learned that making money comes at a price. The price of NOT being able to always do what you love. The price of NOT being able to be completely true to yourself.

We learned that it's impossible to do whatever we feel like if we want to make money. We learned that we have to sacrifice something, if only a little, to make a living. We have to sacrifice our time, our energy, and perhaps some happiness, too.

We learned that when we want more, we have to work harder. There's a higher price to pay and a bigger sacrifice to make.

We learned we can't just do what we love and feel like doing. It's impossible to make money by just being true to ourselves and doing what we love. That can't be!

But it can. The way to be happy and thrive is to be *completely* true to yourself and do what you love in ways that you love. And yes, the money you need will follow as well, someway, somehow!

The more *you* thrive, the more your *business* thrives, too! And the way to make that happen is to become even more who you already are.

Introvert Introspections:

- If you trusted and believed that ALL you have to do to thrive and be happy is to be true to YOURSELF, what would change?
- What would you do?
- What would you stop doing?

If you need more tools to handle obstacles and fears, check out my book *Unmute Your Life - break free from fear & go for what you REALLY want.* In it, you'll find lots of different tools and exercises to move through any fear or obstacle. You can find it here: www.unmuteyourlife.com

In Conclusion

Creating a business and life that are ideal for you is an ongoing process. It may take a while before everything feels ideal for you, depending on how much you need to change. Take your time. There's no need to rush. Even the smallest change will make you feel better. If you continue making (small) improvements, your business (and life) will become more and more perfect for you. Keep taking one step after the other and you *will* succeed.

Don't expect your business to be ideal overnight. Don't force yourself to go fast or meet a deadline. The more pressure you put on yourself, the worse you feel. The more space you give yourself, the better you feel. Just start and keep going. That's all you have to do!

Some steps require more time, others can be taken in minutes. Completely changing your business model will take longer than delegating one more task to your assistant, for example. Try to break all changes down to small and doable steps. Focus on one action at a time. Start with the action that calls you, that seems most logical, that feels easiest, or, if you can't choose, with a random action. And keep taking steps after that.

The most important thing is to pay attention to what you *feel*. Notice what feels good and what doesn't. Notice what lights you up and what brings you down. Notice what energizes and what drains you. If something doesn't feel 100 percent good, ask yourself: what would feel good instead? Act on the answer you get as best you can. Pay attention to this daily.

Ask yourself before you take action, make a decision, or implement an idea: what would make this *completely* ideal for me? What would make this exciting and fun? In an ideal world where everything is possible, everything always works out for me, and nothing scares me: what would I choose then?

I ask myself these questions about *everything* I do. For example, when I create a new online course, I ask myself: what feels best for me? What does the most ideal version of this course look like? What makes it so exciting that I can't wait to create and deliver this course? What would make me want to sign up for this course myself?

Every action, idea, or decision is a "HELL YES!," a "HELL NO!," or a "maybe." When something is a "hell yes" you do it, when it's a "hell no" you don't. When something is a maybe, ask yourself: what needs to change for this to become a "hell yes"? Make the necessary changes. If you can't find a way to feel 100 percent good about something, either ditch it, delegate it, OR change your attitude and perspective toward it. Pay attention to your yesses, nos, and maybes daily, and watch your business and life transform. Paying attention to what you *really* want may feel like extra work in the beginning, but it pays off from the start! And before you know it, tuning into your true desires and making them real becomes your default state.

Finally, know that creating your ideal business and life is not a onetime endeavor that, once finished, is done forever. Your circumstances change, you change, your business changes, your desires change, the world changes. What's ideal for you now may differ from what's ideal for you next month or next year. Keep paying attention to how you feel. Your feelings always tell you when something is off and needs your attention.

I've made so many changes to what felt ideal and exciting before. I stopped delivering online programs that I used to LOVE because I no longer felt excited about them. I changed my prices, my business model, and the way I delivered my services several times. I revamped a lot even *after* I turned myself into a happy hermit. I'm always open to readjust because I'm committed to my freedom, my happiness, and to living a life I love.

There's always more freedom, happiness, and joy available to you. There's no limit to how well you can feel and how good life can get!

In a Nutshell: The Five Steps to Create a Business and Life You Love and Thrive as an Introvert Entrepreneur

1. Decide what you want and commit to doing what it takes to let it unfold.
2. Let the universe handle the details and logistics. Your job is to follow your intuition and do what you know deep down you have to do.
3. Always be true to YOURSELF in everything you do.
4. Say YES to what you love (and do more of that).
5. Say NO to what you don't love. Don't do it, delegate it, or stop fighting it.

Keep faith, keep imagining that what you want is already yours, and keep following your intuition and inner nudges.

Divinely Selfish Declarations

These affirmations can inspire you to stay true to yourself and to your path. Notice which affirmations resonate with you. Write them in your journal, read them regularly, or post them somewhere you'll see them regularly. When you read the affirmations, focus on how they make you *feel*.

Another way to work with affirmations is to pick one and use that as a journal prompt. Write down the affirmation and then write every thought that comes up next. What does this affirmation ignite in you? What does it make you think of? How does it make you feel?

- I am grateful for the happiness, freedom, and abundance I already enjoy, and I allow myself to receive even more!
- All I have to do is to follow my intuition every day, and my ideal business and life will automatically fall into place.
- I allow myself to have a business and life that are 100 percent ideal for me. It's truly okay to have it all and not settle for anything less!
- I give myself permission to be all that I am, to want whatever I want, and to receive it, too!
- All I have to do is to be all that I am.
- I become more of who I truly am each day!
- I'm the boss of my life, my business and myself, and I decide how I choose to live.

- I always listen to my intuition and what I know deep down. I trust that more than anything and anyone else!
- I am powerful, courageous, and strong. I can do anything I set my mind to!
- Whatever feels right and / or light is always what's right for me.
- I am worthy simply because I AM.
- I'm the only one who knows what's right for me.
- Whatever I believe will work for me is what will work for me. My belief makes it so.
- When my inner world is in order, my desired outer results will fall into place.
- My ideal clients are attracted to me because of who I am, exactly as I am. They love me and want to work with me because I am completely true to myself!
- The more I thrive, the more my business thrives.
- I'm committed to my happiness, freedom, and living a life I love!
- I don't exist to serve my business. My business exists to serve me.
- There's no limit to how well I can feel and how good life can get.
- There's always more freedom, space, joy, happiness and love available to me.
- There's always a way to do business my way!

You can sign up to receive a PDF with these Divinely Selfish Declarations (and other gifts) here: www.bookfreebees.com

Blog: My Personal Story— A Message From The Cave

This is the blog I mentioned in Part One, *Chapter 11, The First Year*. I published it on my website on November 23, 2012. In this blog, I announced my decision to turn myself from a crappy hermit to a happy hermit.

I copy/pasted it from my website and did not make any additional edits to it.

———

This article is a personal story.

It's about something I've been struggling with for years (my entire life, really). And it strongly presented itself again in the past couple of months.

The reason I choose to share this with you, even though it feels a bit vulnerable and uncomfortable, is because I think reading my story can be helpful to you.

I don't want to waste your time, so before I dive into it I'll first help you determine if my story might be relevant to you.

My story will probably inspire you if you:

- Always felt different than the people around you. You didn't quite understand them and how they (inter)acted. You often felt like you didn't fit in (and still feel that way from time to time). It's like someone forgot to hand you the manual to social interactions and how the world works when you were born;

- Are someone who feels that what you have to offer is weird, or strange, and you feel pressure (from others or yourself) to adjust or adapt, and you don't want to but don't know how to make your business work YOUR way;
- Are an introvert and / or HSP (highly sensitive person) just like me.

So, here's my story for those of you who are still here:

If you know me or have been reading my ezine for a while, you've probably heard me refer to my "inner hermit" before or heard me call myself a hermit. (Hence the "message from the cave" above this article—I kinda liked that joke myself. ;-))

The reason I feel I am a hermit is because I am both extremely introverted and highly sensitive—great attributes for a coach, but not so great attributes for fitting into society (Or living a life like most people do. Or building a business like most entrepreneurs do.)

My energy drains from social interaction and even from just being around people.

And yes, this also happens even if the activity is something I truly enjoy and I really like the people I'm with. (If you recognize this, you are most likely an introvert as well.)

Of course, every introvert has extrovert moments and vice versa. I'm not a complete lunatic living on the edge of society without ever talking to anyone but myself and my cat. (That I don't even have. ;-))

But if I want to be able to function, be happy, and healthy AND be able to fulfill my mission, I need to spend between 75–90 percent of my time alone. As you can probably imagine, achieving this in a society that is completely built and structured around extroverted people, who thrive on being around people, social activities, and interaction, is a REALLY tough job.

Over the years I have learned how to deal with this. I learned how to manage my energy, how to restore myself when I was drained, how to set boundaries, how to say NO, etc.

I also learned how to structure my business, my programs, my services, and my marketing in a way that works for me. (Which was also a challenge. A lot of the things most business coaches teach don't work for me.)

This year my business grew a lot, and much faster than I expected. Which is of course wonderful news and I am very, very grateful for it.

But … as a result I had too little time for myself again. I felt stressed, completely drained, unhappy, and totally disconnected from my soul and the world—which is how I always feel when I don't spend enough time alone.

I asked myself:

How the hell am I going to take good care of myself, make sure I have plenty of time to be alone, make plenty of money, reach more people, have way less social interaction, publish my book, and launch two new programs in 2013—all at the same time?!!

And for the gazillionth time, I wondered WHY I had such a weird and seemingly contradictory combination of my mission and my personality:

- I need to be alone most of the time yet I work with people.
- I don't want to leave the house and I hate to travel yet it's my mission to reach millions of people worldwide.
- I want to make a difference in the lives of so many people, yet I can only have interactions with clients for a very limited amount of time.
- I love coaching people but it completely drains my energy if I have too many clients.

I slowly found my answer this year, and made a powerful decision as a result of it. I decided to structure my business in a way that serves my inner hermit for 100 percent instead of 90 percent, just as I have already done in my personal life.

This decision means that in 2013 I will only have interactions with clients for a maximum of four hours a week, spread out over two days. (These client hours include any kind of interaction I have with my clients and potential clients: coaching sessions, group calls, teleseminars, sales conversations etc.)

The rest of the time I can develop and launch two new programs, work on my business and marketing, publish and launch my new book, etc., etc.

Right now, I am restructuring my business and programs to make this decision a reality.

I can only do this now, after I learned how to apply marketing and business principles to my business in a way that worked for me. But the most important reason I am now able to do it MY WAY for 100 percent without making any compromises, is this:

Because I finally accepted and embraced my inner hermit completely, and to acknowledge it as my gift and my strength instead of seeing it as a burden I had to work around.

Some of the lessons I've learned that I truly and deeply hope are helpful to you as well, are:

Every aspect of who you truly are has value and is something that in one way or another helps you fulfill your purpose and be the best version of yourself you can possibly be—even those aspects that you think are weird, painful, or a burden to yourself and / or others.

It is entirely possible to be a hermit or an introvert and run a successful business at the same time. Being an entrepreneur gives you the freedom to structure your life and your work in a way that serves you 100 percent—especially when you are an introvert!

Enjoy, share, and celebrate your uniqueness! It is your gift to the world.

I hope reading my story inspired and served you. Be YOU, and build your ENTIRE business and life around it!

What's next?

I hope this book gave you insights and ideas to improve your business and life. I wish you all the happiness and freedom in the world, and then some! I deeply believe that the more people are true to their soul and do what they love, the better off the world is. (And you'll definitely be happier!)
If you're looking for more inspiration or support, I've got you covered.

First, you can get complimentary gifts, which include a PDF with Follow What Feels Good Daily Journal Prompts, an Ideal Schedule Worksheet, and a collection of Divinely Selfish Declarations here: www.bookfreebees.com

If you'd like to learn more about my online programs or how I can support you via private coaching, check out my programs, products, and services here: www.programsandmore.com

An overview of all my books can be found here:
www.booksbybrigitte.com

And come say hi on social media! You can find me here:
Instagram: www.instagram.com/brigitte_van_tuijl/
Facebook: www.facebook.com/brigittevantuijl.artofdivineselfishness/
Twitter: www.twitter.com/brigittevanT

Thank you for reading and playing with this book. I hope you enjoyed it and if so, please leave me a brilliant review! Or just a nice one. That'll make me happy, too. :-)

For now, I wish you all the best, and good luck creating the business and life of your dreams!

Love,

Brigitte

Other Books by Brigitte

The Gap - bridge the space between where you are and where you want to be
No matter how big your dream or goal is, realizing it can be easier than you think. This book shows you how.

The Inner Minimalist - clear the clutter of your mind for a simpler, quieter and happier life
A guide to easily clear your mind for more (inner) freedom and happiness!

Write Your Non-Fiction Book in 3 Months (in only 30 minutes per day!)
This book shows you how to go from book idea to finished first draft in only three months.

The Art of Divine Selfishness Series

Book One: *Unmute Your Life - break free from fear & go for what you REALLY want*
This book helps you uncover your TRUE dreams and make them real.

Book Two: *The Art of Divine Selfishness - transform your life, your business & the world by putting YOU first*
If you want to create a business and life you adore, you need to put yourself first! This book shows you how.

Books in Dutch

Ontdek wat je écht wilt en maak daar (je) werk van
Een praktisch en inspirerend werkboek om zelfstandig in kaart te brengen wat je écht wilt—en daar je werk van te maken.

You can find more information on these and upcoming books at www.booksbybrigitte.com